Glitterworlds

Part of the Goldsmiths Press Future Media series

The Goldsmiths Press Future Media series encourages authors to offer a relatively short, sharp intervention in response to actual or potential short-term, utilitarian and instrumentalist thinking about a particular scenario or performance of media and technological futurism. Our emphasis on feminist, queer, trans, anti-racist and/or speculative approaches to media and technological futures calls for alternatives to TED thinking.

Glitterworlds

The Future Politics of a Ubiquitous Thing

Rebecca Coleman

Goldsmiths
Press

Contents

Figures

Acknowledgements

This book has been a long time in the making. Thanks to Sarah Kember for initially asking me to write a book, many years ago, and for being patient and accommodating of the various iterations it has taken. Thanks to my wonderful colleagues at Goldsmiths and beyond, who encouraged me to think about and write on glitter (and didn't judge me for it) and have given me links, examples and gifts, some of which have found their way into the pages of the book: Kat Jungnickel, Michaela Benson, Ella Harris, Nina Wakeford, Carolyn Pedwell, Liz Moor, Sarah Keenan, Melissa Nolas, Jayne Osgood, Clare Stanhope, Meredith Jones and Yasmina Reggad. A much wider group of people has also supported me in writing this book, whether directly through discussions about it, or through otherwise inspiring me to keep going with it: Carolyn Pedwell (again!), Tara Page, Monica Moreno Figueroa, Jen Tarr, Dorthe Staunæs, Susanna Paasonen, Vikki Bell, Helen Palmer, Anna Hickey-Moody, Nirmal Puwar, Yasmin Gunaratnam, Hettie Malcomson, Bev Skeggs, Celia Lury, Davina Cooper, Alejandra Energici, Elaine Swan. Goldsmiths Press have been great to work with. Thank you to Adriana Cloud, Liron Zisser and especially Ellen Parnavelas and Guy Sewell, who have been accomodating and inventive throughout the production of the book. Thank you to the young women who participated in the collaging workshops in 2016, through which my interest in glitter was sparked. Lou Coleman, Emily Coleman, Rita George and Phil Coleman have provided essential support, not least childcare and cups of tea. The book would not be here without you – thank you.

I have tried out some of the ideas in this book with students on the MA Gender, Sexuality and Media module and MA Feminist Methods Masterclass module at Goldsmiths. Thanks for being open, engaged and constructively critical. I've also talked about and worked with glitter in the *How to do sociology with...* glitter workshop, Methods Lab, Goldsmiths, November 2018, run with Jayne Osgood; the Affective Methodologies workshop at Aarhus University, Denmark, September 2018; the Social Life of Time Conference, Edinburgh, June 2018; the Gender, Sexuality and the Sensory Symposium, University of Kent, May 2017; and the Debates in New

Materialisms conference, Kingston/Central St Martins, September 2016. Thanks to the organisers of and participants in these events for making me sharpen my understanding of glitter, its politics and its temporalities. Max Liboiron and :mentalKLINIK kindly granted copyright to include their images in the Coda. The reviewers of the manuscript, including Anya Galli Robertson and Gay Hawkins, who waived their anonymity, engaged with the argument carefully and constructively. In trying to respond to (most of) their comments, the version that is published is greatly improved. I would like to thank them for their time, sensitivity and insight.

Parts of Chapters 2 and 3 have been published as 'Glitter: a methodology of following the material', in Rebecca Coleman, Tara Page and Helen Palmer (eds) (2019) 'Feminist new materialist practice: the mattering of method', special issue of *MAI: Journal of Feminist Visual Culture*, Issue 4.[1]

The book is dedicated to Sam and Ray: instigators of change.

---

1 Available at https://maifeminism.com/glitter-a-methodology-of-following-the-material/.

Introduction: Glitterworldings and Future Politics I

Glitter's applications are limitless ... In plastics, glitter is molded into a myriad of products and displays. The cosmetic industry relies on glitter as a colorant for nail polish, gel based formulations, and powders. The toy industry uses glitter flocked into fabrics, molded into plastics and suspended in solutions. Glitter enhances the world's finest greeting cards, and is used by screen printers worldwide to add a touch of sparkle to fabrics and paper. [It] is also used by the world's leading bass boat manufacturers to create the unique finish demanded by boating enthusiasts. Let's not forget the millions of Christmas balls and holiday decorations that are adorned with glitter. Parade float designers, theatrical set designers and Mardi Gras creators all use glitter to catch the eye. Loved by children and adults the world over, ... glitter is packaged for use by school supply distributors and craft companies across the globe. (Meadowbrook Inventions, cited by Hibou 2011).

Glitter is ubiquitous. In the first decades of the twenty-first century, glitter is everywhere, from crafting to make-up, vagazzling to glitter-bombing, fashion to fish. Consider, for example, how glitter is described by Meadowbrook Inventions (above), the 'inventor of modern glitter', as being in use worldwide and as having 'limitless' applications. Glitter also gets everywhere. It sticks to what it is and isn't intended to, and travels beyond its original uses, eliciting affects and emotions from delight to irritation. This book examines this dual sense of the ubiquity of glitter, following glitter as it moves across different sites, or worlds.

Throughout the book is a concern with how the movement of glitter in and across different worlds is transformational and future-oriented. As it moves, glitter makes worlds, it brings these worlds to life. This worlding is a process that is unsettled, or open-ended. Glitter has the capacity to world differently, to create a variety of futures. I argue that the movement and sticking of glitter and the making and changing of worlds generates a range of politics. Such a politics requires an attention to the specificities of how glitter worlds. Indeed, while a predominant way in which glitter is reported on today is in terms of the environmental damage it does and that it therefore should be banned, this is only one of a multiplicity of politics that glitter is involved in. LGBTQ* glitter-bombing is another, as are embodied and decorative practices involving the material, and how it does, and does not, become an enchanting material via which differently racialised young women can imagine their futures. In diversifying the politics of glitter, it is not always immediately self-evident what 'politics' is, and how it is manifested. In exploring some of the political questions that glitter generates, my focus is on how particular futures are fabricated, or fabulated. That is, as unfinished, changing, and in-the-making, glitter worldings are directed towards that which is not yet, as well as what is. The title of the book, then, seeks to capture the ways in which glitter is involved in worldings, how these worldings are specific and unfinished, and how these specific and unfinished glitter worldings are oriented around both the present and future.

This introductory chapter is divided into three sections. In the first section, I explain what I mean by 'glitterworlds', and in particular emphasise their ongoingness and unfinishedness. To express this processual quality of glitterworlds, I introduce the notion of glitterworld*ings*, where the emphasis is on dynamism and transformation. The second part of the chapter outlines the conceptual framework that I assemble in order to understand these glitterworlds. I explain how I aim to bring together feminist cultural theory, feminist new materialisms and recent work on temporality and futures to grasp the politics that glitter generates. In the third section, I provide an overview of the book, drawing out key themes that it covers, and pointing to some areas that it doesn't. In addition to providing a map of the book, then, the second and third sections seek to make clear the aims of the book, and the kind of intervention it tries to make in some of the dominant ways in which glitter is reported on in mainstream media.

Glitterworlds, Glitterworldings

In this book, the term 'glitterworlds' has at least three, interconnected, senses. In one sense, the term 'glitterworlds' seeks to capture the ways in which glitter moves across different domains. Worlds refer to the distinct situations in which glitter becomes significant. Thus, glitter's role in

LGBTQ* culture is understood as a 'world', as is how it features as a filmic device, as is how it moves into marine life. The book *follows glitter across different worlds*, exploring how these worlds are both distinct, and share similiarities.

In a second sense, the term is attentive to *the particularities of glitter in making particular worlds*. In this sense, the materiality and mediation of glitter is significant. In her study of the new technology of glass in the eighteenth century, Isobel Armstrong (2008) coins the term 'glassworlds' to understand both the material and imaginary worlds that glass gave life to, arguing that 'Victorian glassworlds provide a material and conceptual site for nineteenth century modernism to play out their concerns' (2008: 16). For Armstrong, glassworlds are a means to analyse how a new material became popular and prevalent, and how it embodied Victorian values including respect and appreciation for new materials and technologies, and of transparency. In both of these cases, glass creates worlds.

Sarah Kember (2016) develops a notion of glassworlds to consider how glass is 'the ubiquitous *i*material of the day' (2016: 32). As it proliferates across the screens of smartphones, tablets, (Google) glasses and kitchens (the '*i*' of *i*materials), Kember argues that it is celebrated as a material that 'has come to incorporate the properties of plastic and is promoted as an intelligent skin, covering and protecting the data subjects, objects and environments of *i*media by making everything (equally) clear, open and transparent' (2016: 32). Kember's focus on glassworlds is important for its understanding of glass as a material that is at once media; that is, her focus is on glass as a ubiquitous material in contemporary digitally mediated cultures. Glass is a ubiquitous material for *i*media environments. Materials are media, and media are materials. Kember's approach to glassworlds is also important for how it unpicks the celebratory framings of glass as *i*media/*i*material, arguing that the seemingly non-hierarchal values of openness and transparency are both mobilised and characterised by masculinist 'industry goals oriented to novelty and innovation' (2016: 24). These accounts tell particular stories about the present or near future that perpetuate technocentric understandings of what materials and media are able – and may yet be able – to do. For example, she notes how objects from Google Glass to care robots are presented as visions for how technology can solve problems in the future in ways that perpetuate existing inequalities concerning gender, sexuality, race, class, age and dis/ability.

Kember critiques these masculinist accounts of the seeming inevitability of technological progress (where progress is understood as linear: read, flowing towards a better future, unhindered by politics or ethics). In such accounts, the future is posited as both exciting and already (technologically) determined. She draws contrasts with feminist SF, drawn especially from Haraway, who attends to the multiplicity of SF:

Sf is that potent material semiotic sign for the riches of speculative fabulation, speculative feminism, science fiction, science fact, science fantasy – and, I suggest, string figures. In looping threads and relays of patterning, this sf practice is a model for worlding. Sf must also mean 'so far', opening up what is yet-to-come in protean times pasts, presents and futures (Haraway 2012: 4, cited in Kember 2016: 29).

For Haraway and Kember, then, the future is both 'not-yet' and in non-linear relations with pasts and presents. The future is capable of being made and made differently, *and* at the same time is looping, threading and relaying with other temporalities. It is neither completely open (exciting) nor closed (inevitable). What is required is close attention to how futures are made and re-made, how worlds are worlded. Indeed, Haraway argues,

it matters what matters we use to think other matters with; it matters what stories we tell to tell other stories with; it matters what knots knot knots, what thoughts think thoughts, what descriptions describe descriptions, what ties tie ties. It matters what stories make worlds, what worlds make stories (2016: 12).

In arguing that 'it matters', Haraway draws attention both to the ethics and politics of worldings, and to the particular materials and media (stories, knots, thoughts, descriptions, ties) via which worldings occur. Both of these senses of her argument are important for this book: my argument is that glitter is a politically and ethically significant thing in diverse and multiple worldings.

As may be becoming apparent, the term 'glitterworlds' has a dynamic sense, in that *glitter does not just move across different sites (glitterworlds) but it helps to make or build these sites.* In other words, the third sense of glitter is that it is lively and energetic, or vibrant. It is part of what constitutes or worlds worlds. Worlds do not exist in quite the same way without glitter as part of their mix. I am not claiming that glitter is the only thing or always the most important thing in the worlds that I analyse in this book, but that in being in, becoming with, these worlds, it changes these worlds. The worlds become, differently, because glitter is part of them. It is in this sense that a *future politics* of glitter emerges. In its dynamism and constitution of worlds, glitter is transformational. In worlding, glitter makes certain futures and not others. These futures are not pre-determined, although they are made in the context of existing economic, social, cultural and environmental processes and practices. An attention to future politics emerges by looking at what worlds glitter worlds, and how.

An Interdisciplinary 'Scholarly Imagination'[1]

The book brings together three ways of thinking about and working with glitter: feminist cultural theory, feminist new materialisms and the emphasis in recent social science and humanities work on futures, especially in Science and Technology Studies (STS). The aim in bringing these sometimes disparate strands of work together is to develop an approach to glitter that can capture its multiplicity and movement. Feminist cultural theory provides me with an understanding of the significance of seemingly mundane and ubiquitous things to the production and organisation of gender, sexuality, race and class. Glitter is often deemed frivolous and even dangerous, and these are qualities that are associated with minoritarian groups. In other words, glitter is seen as feminine, childish, queer. I also explore how some of the qualities of glitter and the ways in which it features in various practices and media emphasise whiteness, arguing that it is therefore necessary to consider how and where glitter generates political questions that are racialised. Feminist cultural theory helps me to take seriously popular culture and to unpack the politics of these associations.

---

1 The term 'scholarly imagination' is from Kara Keeling (2019), as I expand on below.

Inflecting feminist cultural theory with feminist new materialist work enables a focus on how *things* are involved in these politics. That is, the book places emphasis on how glitter *as a thing* produces and organises gender, sexuality, race, class and age. Understanding glitter as a thing draws on work in the social sciences and puts this together with feminist new materialist approaches that complicate the divisions between nature and culture by seeing agency – life and liveliness – as distributed across humans and non-humans, rather than only as the preserve of the human. I therefore link social scientific work that has focused on things and feminist new materialist work, arguing that while the approach that I develop is not unproblematic or complete (as I discuss below), it draws attention to the role that things may have in generating politics that disturb the now and create alternatives.

More specifically, my focus on things seeks to capture how glitter functions as both material and media. The connection I make between feminist cultural theory and feminist new materialisms highlights how things are in constant movement and transformation. Work from both of these fields sees this dynamism as central to media and culture and to materials and matter. Moreover, both feminist cultural theory and feminist new materialisms help to rethink the boundaries between media and materials; as I argue, thingness is both material and immaterial, a series of properties and communicative capacities. Things are affective, mediating and communicating sensations that are felt and lived out materially. As I have noted, glitter as a thing moves, and my focus on things is explicated not only theoretically or conceptually but also methodologically in that the book *follows* glitter as it moves across, transforms and makes worlds. The method of following the thing, then, is developed through approaches that see the vibrancy and vitality of things as requiring an approach that is itself mobile and capable of attending to material sensations. This is another reason for elaborating an account of glitter as both media and material – as thing – in that it is necessary to consider how glitter, as it worlds, is not so much representational or symbolic as felt, embodied and changing.

The emphasis I place on glitter as moving and transformational indicates that as a thing glitter is unfinished and open-ended. It keeps moving. Both feminist cultural theory and feminist new materialisms see politics as, in part, involved in the creation of futures that are different to and better than the past. This is at least part of the impetus of feminist, queer and anti-racist work. In attending to the politics of glitter I am especially interested in how these politics are future-oriented, or oriented to making more desirable futures. In this sense, the book contributes to a recent resurgence of interest in temporality and futures, where Tavia Nyong'o (2019) notes, 'the onto-epistemological question of what time is, in other words, has come increasingly to the fore in ongoing interdisciplinary debates' (2019: 21). Nyong'o's focus is on queer Black life, and he proposes a concept of 'Afro-fabulation' to draw out the poetics of how such life is sustained and invented. In so doing, time is understood as relational, a kind of '*in media res*' (Nyong'o 2019: 5) that 'tethers together worlds that can and cannot be, and is thus a necessary step toward investigating possibilities outside our present terms of order' (2019: 6).

Afro-fabulation for Nyong'o, and fabulation for other writers, is a way to consider how futures and presents are intimately attached, and how the future holds the promise of something different (which may already be a potential within the present). Moreover, fabulation refers to a process via which new futures are created via mediators, which might be people, works of art or things. I develop an account of fabulation whereby glitter is a mediator for the creation of new futures. Futures are the not-yet and at the same time are felt and anticipated in, and oriented around, the present. Temporality is thus not linear or progressive but intensive, affective, multiple. Importantly, then, *following* glitter involves a concentration on how glitter *fabulates* worlds. Following glitter is not necessarily or only a tracing of the linear unfolding of the future, but rather a movement with how glitter worlds through its scatterings, spreadings, stickings and stayings.

It is significant, I think, that Nyong'o sees the increasing attention to temporality as interdisciplinary; in putting together feminist cultural theory, feminist new materialisms and social science work on futures and temporality, I am attempting to create a productive space in which to understand some of the political questions that I see as generated through a practice of following glitter. In her work on queer and Black futures, Kara Keeling (2019), quoting Stuart Hall's (1990) characterisation of the work of the Birmingham Centre for Contemporary Cultural Studies (CCCS), calls this a mode of scholarly production that imaginatively, yet seriously, engages with disciplinary and interdisciplinary areas' 'existing paradigms and traditions of knowledge' and 'empirical and concrete work' to construct a new scholarly terrain. Such an endeavour is calibrated to 'be of service to people studying' a particular object or set of objects, or to those interested in specific questions; it creates ways to do that work. It is animated by a scholarly imagination. (2019: 11)

Hall sees such an endeavour as inventive, in that it is a bringing-into-being of something that did not already exist. Here, both the novelty of the CCCS's ways of working and the process through which these ways of working were generated can be understood as inventive. That is, the endeavour as well as the results are 'animated by a scholarly imagination'. Moreover, as indicated by the explanation of the 'mode of scholarly production' as in the service of particular objects, sets of objects and specific questions, this inventiveness is ongoing; the way of working is not generalisable but must be tailored to that which is to be understood (see also Coleman 2009, 2017a). To understand the future politics of glitter as it pertains to questions of gender, sexuality, race, class and age, then, has required me to think together sometimes inconsistent strands of thought.

Keeling's argument regarding the 'scholarly imagination' is also important in how she sees it as in contrast to the ways in which the future, and especially scenario building, has become central to capitalist knowledge production (see 2019: 1–40). While it is impossible to draw hard and fast lines between the university and corporate knowledge production, in ways that resonate with the work of Haraway and Kember discussed above, Keeling proposes that the imagination that animates scholarly work is political and ethical in being a 'generative, deterritorialising' force (2019: 16). Whereas the futures imagined by commercial corporations are necessarily profit-driven, the scholarly imagination is able to conjure alternatives to capitalist organisations. While commercial corporations begin from and reproduce capitalist socio-political life, the scholarly imagination can

challenge the processes of commensuration built into the demand for [a minoritarian] group to become perceptible according to existing conceptions of the world. It is a way of asserting the existence in this world of another conception of the world, incomprehensible from within the common senses that secure existing hegemonic relations and their 'computations of relative value.' (Keeling 2019: 31; see also Coleman 2017b)

In other words, the scholarly imagination can conceive of a world outside of the dominant ways in which it exists now. At the same time, it can point to how this alternative world already exists in ways that challenge majoritarian modes of organisation, opening up the possibilities of more fundamental change. Throughout the book is an attempt to explore the temporal dimensions of the politics that this scholarly imagination suggests through the study of glitter. My aim in doing this is to avoid a techno-centrist understanding of the future as that which inevitably and unavoidably proceeds from the past and present, ultimately culminating in social progress. In so doing, I seek to draw attention to alternative futures that may and may not be understood in terms of progress; the better futures that I am interested in are specific and particular, requiring a focus on not only for whom and how the future is better, but also how futures may not unfurl smoothly but may involve shock, surprise and sometimes aspirations to what is considered normal and often problematic (Berlant 2007). The future politics I am interested in, then, are plural as well as particular; multiple, diverse and always in the process of changing.

Following Glitter; Configuring the Book

There are limits on the future politics of glitter that this book follows. Most obviously, what the book does not do is examine in detail the politics that are generated through what glitter does after its involvement in everyday activities, as it becomes waste. This is a particularly important point to make given the widespread attention that is rightly focused on the environmental effects of plastics, including glitter. In Chapter 2, I discuss both the importance and some of the pitfalls of understanding glitter predominantly in terms of plastics-as-waste. There, drawing on STS approaches to plastic, waste and politics, I explore the temporalities (and especially futures) through which understandings of the politics of plastics-as-waste function and argue that other politics are also necessary to examine. I suggest that framings of glitter as wasteful and having negative effects on the natural environment tend to work through fears of the future – affects that are at odds with the ways in which glitter is more readily associated with fun, frivolity, magic and enchantment. Indeed, as the epigraph from Meadowbrook Inventions indicates, glitter is 'loved by children and adults the world over'. Contemporary marketing of products involving glitter similarly evoke these more joyful affects, as tubes of glitter for crafting are described as 'wonderful' and 'vivid', biodegradable glitter for faces and bodies as 'glamourous' and 'fun' and glittery shoes and boots as 'light-catching, attention-grabbing'. Self-help books are also capitalising on such ideas, with titles such as *A Life Full of Glitter: A Guide to Positive Thinking, Self-Acceptance, and Finding Your Sparkle in a (Sometimes) Negative World* (O'Brien 2018), *Be More Unicorn: How to Find Your Inner Sparkle* (Gray 2018) and *Shine: Rediscovering Your Energy, Happiness and Purpose* (Cope and Oattes 2018), all published recenty. These diverse examples highlight the associations between glitter, wonder and transformation, which contrast with the more dystopian affects around which campaigns and reports focused on nature and the environment are organised.

Throughout the book, I attempt to consider how 'cultural' and 'environmental' politics are always entangled. Alongside this thread is the argument that to focus squarely on the environmental politics of glitter is to miss the multiple and at times contradictory ways in which glitter is experienced and engaged. In many ways, to focus on environmental politics at the expense of cultural politics is to sideline the question of why and how glitter has such a ubiquity at the moment, despite the environmental problems it creates. To make clear, my point here is not that research on and campaigns about the environmental effects of glitter are unimportant, inaccurate or worthless; it is necessary to demonstrate that plastics *are* wasteful and have detrimental impacts on many different human and non-human entities. Rather, my aim is to highlight the array of affects and effects through which glitter is currently understood and experienced and to complicate the idea of a pure nature being contaminated by artificial culture. Nature and culture, bodies and objects, media and materials are entangled – or, perhaps put more forcefully – are fabulated together. The creation, mass production and consumption of new artificial materials – such as plastic – helps to constitute what nature 'is' as they move 'into' it. In developing her concept of trans-corporeality, Stacy Alaimo explores the 'traffic in toxins' between humans and non-humans, arguing that it makes it difficult to 'imagine that it is possible to protect "nature" by merely creating separate, distinct areas in which it is "preserved" ' (2010: 18). Instead, she argues that the movement of toxins across different bodies and environments 'mixes things up':

Since the same chemical substance may poison the workers who produce it, the neighbourhood in which it is produced, and the web of plants and animals who end up consuming it, the traffic in toxins reveals the interconnections among various movements, such as environmental health, occupational health, labour, environmental justice, popular epidemiology, environmentalism, ecological medicine, disability rights, green living, antiglobalisation, consumer rights, and children's health and welfare (2010: 18).

In addition to the discussion of plastic in Chapter 2, in Chapter 4 I focus on the practices of vagazzling and vagina glitter bombs and explore how glitter is framed by medics and cultural commentators as an artificial material that potentially pollutes the natural body. However, I also complicate the idea of the 'natural body', unpacking the class-based assumptions of what is appropriate to go on and in bodies, and suggesting that working-class women are more likely than middle-class women to be seen as indulging in unsuitable activities. In other words, what is considered a natural body is constructed through a cultural politics of class. In the intervention called *Identifying* included towards the end of the book, I also examine the intricate relations between nature and culture through a consideration of how plastics move into marine life and may – and may not – be identified as pollutants, and the ways in which the production of glitter and sustainable alternatives such as mica have bodily effects on those who mine them.

In exploring the cultural as well as environmental politics of glitter, I seek to emphasise the seriousness of seemingly frivolous things. For example, consider an article in the *Guardian* with the headline 'Angry about Brexit? David Cameron's smiling festival selfies definitely won't help' (Pass Notes 2018a). The piece is illustrated with a selfie of the Conservative prime minister of the United Kingdom from 2010 to 2016 surrounded by a hen party of white women wearing glitter make-up on their faces and a photograph of him being hugged by a person in a glittery jacket with 'Corbyn' (the name of the then Labour leader) written on the back. The photographs were taken at the middle-class festival Wilderness in 2018 and 2017 respectively. The article goes on to note that '[t]he ex-PM loves swanning around Wilderness, cocktail in hand', rather than 'sitting at home contemplating the wreckage of his life and country as we would wish him to'. Similar photographs illustrate articles and reports on glitter, plastic and the natural environment, as I discuss in Chapter 2. In these senses, glitter functions as a counterfoil to more serious politics – of national politics and of the planet. While these serious politics are certainly that – serious – their construction as such through the juxtaposition of glitter as frivolous is problematic when gender, sexuality, race, class and age are in focus. That is, the seriousness of the politics of glitter encompasses rather than excludes the frivolousness of cultural politics. Moreover, as is evident throughout the book, the distinction between frivolousness and seriousness does not hold when the politics of glitter are at stake. As Susan Sontag (1966/2018) puts it, and as I discuss in more detail in Chapter 6, '[o]ne can be serious about the frivolous, frivolous about the serious' (2018: 26).

The serious-frivolous politics of glitter constitute a central line of analysis throughout the book. In Chapter 1, I outline what following glitter involves, developing the conception of things as both theoretical and methodological, and as both media and material. In this chapter, I come back to why I find it helpful to bring together feminist cultural theory and feminist new materialisms, and consider some of the risks of so doing, especially in terms of what Kember terms the potential for a focus on things to become 'compatible, if not necessarily complicit with, industry goals oriented to novelty and innovation – iPhones[n] – rather than invention and intervention' (2016: 24). Chapter 2 focuses on the future politics of glitter, examining, as I've indicated above, the prevalent ways in which glitter is seen in terms of a politics of plastic-as-waste. The central aim of this chapter is not to dislodge the importance of the environmental effects of plastic so much as to demonstrate a plurality of politics. This chapter also introduces in detail the central concept of fabulation that is returned to and re-turned (Hughes and Lury 2013) in Chapters 3–6 and its relationships to the concepts of hope and pre-figurative politics. All of these, in different but intersecting ways, draw attention to how better futures are imagined, engaged and brought into being and to the non-linear relations between presents and futures. They are the ways in which I see a following of glitter as an attention to the ways in which glitter makes worlds.

Chapters 3–6 develop these ideas through empirically following glitter to different sites, or worlds. Chapter 3 focuses on workshops with teenage girls, where they collaged imaginations of their futures. Out of a range of materials that I provided for the collaging, glitter emerged as particularly popular. In this chapter, I attempt to understand this popularity of glitter, linking it to mainstream girls' culture, and specifically to what Mary Celeste Kearney (2015) calls 'luminosity', a visual convention whereby girls and young women in contemporary media culture are illuminated through shimmer and sparkle. Taking up this visual practice of luminosity, I analyse some of the collages made in the workshops and, drawing through the methodological aspect of following the thing outlined in Chapter 1, I also consider the collaging workshops as a method in which the conditions to imagine – or fabulate – futures are created.

Chapters 4 and 5 continue the focus on the relationships between young women, luminosity and glitter. In Chapter 4, I follow glitter to two bodily practices: vagazzling, where crystals, glitter and other decorative accessories are glued onto a shaved mons pubis, and vagina glitter bombs, where capsules filled with glitter are inserted into the vagina and then melt, making vaginal fluids sparkle. In focusing on these two examples, I explore their roots in celebrity culture and media debates about them, considering how they move between and complicate the boundaries between the inside and outside of the body, private and public, and nature and culture. I understand them as practices through which glitter functions as both media, in its abilities to communicate something intimate, and as material, as a substance that as it moves between and across nature and culture. In so doing, I consider the politics of glitter as it becomes contested for the harms and pleasures it may bring.

Chapter 5 moves to explore glitter as it functions as filmic devices in the films *Glitter* (2001) and *Precious – based on the novel Push by Sapphire* (2009). While distinctly different genres of film – the former, featuring Mariah Carey as the main character, deemed a box office flop and the latter a critical success with white audiences – both illuminate a racial politics of glitter and luminosity that is organised in terms of presents and futures. On the face of it, *Glitter* tells the story of the incredible success

of its mixed-race protagonist Billie Frank as she becomes an internationally recognised singer, seemingly unfurling a better future from a painful
past. However, I argue that the temporalities of the film are more complicated than this, as Billie constantly moves between the past, present and
future, and the better future she arrives at the end of the film is tempered
by loss and ambivalence. *Precious* follows the main character of the same
name, an African-American sixteen-year-old who is excluded from school
for being pregnant for the second time by her father, joins an alternative
school, learns to read and write and forges friendships and a sense of
selfhood. As with *Glitter*, *Precious* can in one way be seen as a movement
towards a better future; however, I explore how a number of cultural, film
and media theorists have debated its progressiveness, arguing instead that
the film encompasses both hope and despair and challenging the ways
Black characters are portrayed and its appeal to white audiences.

Of central importance to this chapter are how in *Precious* fantasy
scenes are a means by which Precious is removed/removes herself from
the abuse she encounters in her present and imagines or experiences an
alternative future. I explore how glitter appears in this film as a device that
indicates a movement or transition between Precious' reality and fantasies, and make connections between this and how glitter functions as a
filmic convention in *Glitter*. I return to the visual practice of luminosity,
examining how it is involved in racialization and, drawing on Nyong'o's
concept of Afro-fabulation, consider the ways in which Billie and Precious
are able to imagine and realise futures different to their presents and pasts.

Chapter 6 extends the focus from girls and young women to LGBTQ*
glitter-bombing activism, where homophobic public figures, including
politicians, and institutions are covered with 'sparkly showers'. In concentrating on activism, this chapter most explicitly explores what may be
called 'serious politics', in that glitter-bombing is a deliberate attempt to
raise awareness, change policy and make better futures. However, many
of the activists explain their actions in terms of the fabulousness of glitter,
linking it to its long history in gay culture, including as a kind of performative politics. Drawing on Sontag's conceptualisation of Camp as both
serious and frivolous, and on the practices of pre-figurative politics as a
means of making the future in and as the present, in this chapter I explore

glitter-bombing as a way of creating a better future through fabulising the present.

The final chapter of the book, the Coda, returns to the interdisciplinary scholarly imagination discussed above, and draws together the issues regarding glitterworldings, future politics and following the thing examined across the book. In particular, I propose an interdisciplinary scholarly imagination that seeks to provide opportunities for the fabulation of futures and to become attuned to how fabulations of futures already exist, even if in minor and apparently unsuccessful ways. As a process, fabulation is necessarily unfinished. To work with this aspect of fabulation, at the end of the book are short interventions that posit some other ways of following glitter. These include further empirical examples of how future politics are being created through glitter, and re-turn to issues raised in earlier chapters. In this way, the book attempts to open out to some of the ways in which it might be developed further by drawing attention to and posing questions that put into play other possible followings and fabulations of glitter – to some of its other possible futures.

1

Following the Thing...

What the ubiquity of media entails, then, is a re-conceptualisation of what it is we mean by the term 'media'. (Steinberg 2009: 114)

Vital materialists will thus try to linger in those moments during which they find themselves fascinated by objects, taking them as clues to the material vitality that they share with them. (Bennett 2010: 17)

We have to follow the things themselves. (Appadurai 1986)

These three epigraphs indicate the central concerns of this chapter, in which I develop a methodological and conceptual understanding of 'things' in order to study glitter. My argument is that to develop an account of things it is necessary to see theory and method as entangled; that is, the conceptual and methodological aspects of 'things' are entwined and co-constitutive. As such, throughout the chapter, I move across and between discussions of theory and method, re-turning (to) points as the analysis develops.

This attempt to enmesh theory and method in the writing of the chapter emerges from approaches to 'follow the things', which have been significant in a range of social science work for the past three decades. While coming from different disciplinary backgrounds and having different aims, what these approaches share is an attempt to trouble what the anthropologist Arjun Appadurai (1986) describes as the 'powerful con-temporary tendency [...] to regard the world of things as inert and mute, set in motion and animated, indeed knowable, only by persons and their words' (1986: 4). For Appadurai, any attempt to correct or reverse this ten-dency is both, at once, a theoretical and methodological project, for he suggests that 'even though from a *theoretical* point of view human actors encode things with significance, from a *methodological* point of view it is the things-in-motion that illuminate their human and social context' (1986: 5, emphasis in original). Indeed, he argues that 'we have to follow the things themselves, for their meanings are inscribed in their forms, their uses, their trajectories' (1986: 5).

The chapter aims to do two primary things. First, it examines how approaches have been developed to *follow* the lives and liveliness of things, exploring how they cut across theory and method. I connect up social science methods of following the thing with research in feminist new materialisms, and especially Jane Bennett's (2010) work on vibrant matter and thing-power. I pay particular attention to the politics and ethics that a methodology of following the thing raises regarding the attention given to matter, materials, things and the relations between humans and non-humans. I suggest that an expansive notion of life that includes non-human things can be productively connected with theories that open out what counts as media through a consideration of the liveliness and lifeness of media, objects and materials.

Second, then, I introduce how the term 'thing' is the way in which I conceive glitter as both material and media. That glitter is a material is in many ways obvious. Glitter is a collection of small, reflective plastic fragments that come in different colours and shapes, reflecting light at various angles so that it sparkles (see Chapter 2 for more on its materiality). What is less clear, though, is how and why glitter might also be a medium. Marc Steinberg expands on his point in the epigraph that, in an age of ubiquitous media, it is necessary to redefine what 'media' refers to by arguing that 'we must begin to understand everyday objects from branded TV shirts to airplanes as media forms unto themselves', thus '[d]isplacing the common-sense, classical communication studies conception of "the media" (as denoting the major mass media of radio, television, film, print)' (Steinberg 2009: 114). In the terms set out by Steinberg here, I ask, might glitter be understood as ubiquitous media in a similar way to branded TV shirts and airplanes? What does an understanding of glitter as ubiquitous offer to such an approach? How does conceiving of glitter as both material *and* media shed light on the ways in which glitter is engaged with in everyday life, and the politics it might generate? I suggest that central in theories of ubiquitous media and the new materialisms and in methodologies of following the thing are vibrancy, movement and transformation. In defining glitter as thing, then, I pick up on the discussion in the Introduction regarding the future-orientation of glitter, and set up following as the methodology through which the book unfolds.

Following the Thing: Movement, Transformation, Affect

Appadurai's proposal of following the thing is situated within a wider argument concerning commodities. His dissatisfaction with an interpretation of things as 'inert and mute' is based on an understanding of commodities as in circulation; in processes of exchange, value and politics. Interestingly, such a conception of commodities leads Appadurai to define commodities as 'things with a particular type of social potential' (1986: 6). However, rather than this potential being the property only of commodities, all things may move in and out of this situation. Hence, he asks us to, 'approach commodities as things in a certain situation, a situation that can characterise many different kinds of thing, at different points in their social lives. This means looking at the commodity potential of all things rather than searching fruitlessly for the magic distinction between commodities and other sorts of things' (1986: 13).

As things with a particular type of social potential that become definitional at a particular point in their social lives, commodities are always in movement. Indeed, in their work on the global culture industry, Scott Lash and Celia Lury (2007) explain that one of the strengths of Appadurai's approach of 'following the thing' is that it prioritises an attention to 'how things actually move, how they "transition" between many states, how they are (self)organised as temporal, rhythmic morphologies or coherent behaviours (Kwinter 2001)' (2007: 19). That is, things are both lively (animated, in motion) and have a life (have trajectories). Such an understanding of things as both lively and with lives indicates that things have the capacity for change. Appadurai explains that the movement of commodities is not necessarily linear, in that 'things can move in *and* out of the commodity state, that such movements can be fast or slow, reversible or terminal, normative or deviant' (1986: 13). As such, movement is potentially both transformational (in that a thing can change into a commodity and back into a thing at multiple points during its life), and looping or folding or slowly proceeding. This movement that characterises a thing is thus processual and open-ended. The life of a thing is to be followed because it is not necessarily clear what movements it will make and how these movements will come to change it, or not.

The propensity of a thing to move and change may be understood not only in terms of its life (its trajectory), but also its liveliness. Indeed, while distinct, these two aspects of a thing cannot be understood in isolation; they are both integral characteristics. Sharing with both Appaadai and Lash and Lury a concern with understanding things as animated and alive in themselves (rather than only as brought to life via human agency), Jane Bennett (2010) develops a vital materialist approach to things. She argues that things have the capacity to 'act as quasi agents or forces with trajectories, propensities, or tendencies of their own' (2010: viii). That is, things have life/are lively in themselves and are not only brought to life via human agency. In this way, the line between animation as a human quality and automation as a non-human quality is challenged (see Stacey and Suchman 2012; Coleman 2014a). 'Thing-power' is Bennett's term for capturing the vibrancy and affectivity of a thing. She explains that '[t]hing-power gestures toward the strange ability of ordinary, man-made items to exceed their status as objects and to manifest traces of independence or aliveness' (2010: xvi). For Bennett, then, things have an agency of their own. While they may be man-made, and hence are in relations with humans, they also have the capacity for autonomy – a life/liveliness that exceeds humans. For example, introducing her conception of vital materials, Bennett discusses how a range of items lying in a gutter – glove, pollen, rat, cap, stick – 'commanded attention in its own right, as existents in excess of their association with human meanings, habits, or projects' (2010: 4). As she goes on to explain, being '*struck*' by these items facilitated an understanding of their 'thing-power': 'At the very least, it provoked affects in me' (2010: 4).

My proposal to understand glitter as *thing* draws on these accounts of the vibrancy and vitality of things. Central to the liveliness and lifeness of things is movement; as I outlined in the Introduction and expand upon below, movement is inherent to the perception and experience of life in general and to plastics and glitter more specifically. Noting that things move and shift, Appadurai and Lash and Lury propose a methodology of following the thing. Indeed, Lash and Lury, drawing on Appadurai, explain that if a thing is followed 'back in time and forward along its biograph- ical trajectory', attention is given to the question of 'how is the object is transformed – and how does it transform – from stage to stage, context to context?' (2007: 16).[1] This is an understanding of the thing 'not as existing ideally in a steady state or condition, but as a set of relations, that is, as always coming into existence' (references omitted, 2005: 17–18; see also Lury 2004). What this implies is that the thing is both capable of trans- formation (becoming) and is in constitutive relations with the conditions through which it emerges. Things and people are embedded in the envir- onments via which things, people and the environments emerge, as Alaimo (2010) among others argues (see Chapter 2). For Lash and Lury, 'our method does not assume a distinction between media and society; our assumption is instead that we live in a media-society, and that the users, producers and circulators of media are not on a separate level to others' (2005: 28). In other words, media are not separate to the social environment but an integral aspect of it.

Following the *Thing*: Materials, Media, Movement

Recent theories of media are helpful to expand on this relationship between things, movement and emergent relationality. As indicated in the epigraph from Steinberg, such approaches open out what counts as 'media', so that media refers not only to 'the media' (typically, broadcast or mass media),

---

1 It is worth noting here that Lash and Lury talk of 'objects' as well as 'things'. My aim here is not to discuss the specific traditions that Lash and Lury draw upon in the development of their methodology, important as they are, so much as to draw out what I see as connections between the various work on things that I discuss here.

but also encompasses everyday objects that in various ways mediate and communicate. Indeed, W.J.T. Mitchell (2017) writes that, '[a]bsolutely anything can become a medium, but that does not mean that everything is functioning as a medium at all times' (2017: 14). In similar ways to how Appadurai sees things as potentially moving in and out of the commodity state, a definition of media is not stable or finished.

This 'predicament of media', as Craig Dworkin (2013: 30) puts it – what is/are (the) media? When is and isn't something media? – is worth examining further. Dworkin's central point in posing the predicament of media is that 'contrary to the casual ways in which we use the term, there is no "medium". No single medium can be apprehended in isolation' (2013: 28). Instead, 'media (always necessarily multiple) only become legible in social contexts because they are not things, but rather activities: commercial, communicative, and, always, interpretative' (2013: 28). These three points – that media are always multiple, that they are activities rather than objects and that they are social, or in social contexts – are mutually constitutive. That media are necessarily multiple draws attention to the material relations and activities via which media function. Taking the CD as an example, Dworkin explains that the ' "medium" of the music, in the sense of its material format', requires a network of materials and devices including a CD player, a laser, a processor, wires, drivers, electricity and a listener (2013: 30). 'However absurdly obvious these requirements sound when enumerated in this way', he points out, 'they are not trivial for a rigourous definition of media' (2013: 30). Furthermore, what this example also indicates is that rather than autonomous objects, media become recognisable through 'social context': 'materials can only be legible as media under certain circumstances; they only make sense in specific contexts. … Particular social milieus make that meaning available' (2013: 30).

The definition of media that Dworkin proposes here challenges a technological determinist version of media and its relationship to the future that, as I discuss below, is critiqued by feminist and queer work. Media do not come from nowhere, and nor do they exist in a vacuum. Rather, media are always socially situated. The futures they may help to bring into being require labour, and hence are not natural or inevitable. Returning to the discussion of materials, above, and the emphasis placed on dynamism (activity) and relationality (social context), this definition of media indicates that both materials and media are understood as changing, becoming and capable of taking on different meanings depending on the contexts and relations they are embedded within and entangled with. Indeed, as Jussi Parikka (2012) notes, much new materialist work is concerned with ' "mediatic" phenomena' (2012: 95), and one of its tasks is 'to be able to talk not only of objects, but also as much about non-solids and the processual' (2012: 99).

According to these definitions, then, glitter may be understood as media. Centrally, as Dworkin points out, glitter is 'commercial, communicative, and, always, interpretative' (2013: 28). It is itself multiple – glitter is a collection of tiny bits of plastic – it has a multiplicity of uses, and, as I explore in this book, it communicates and is interpreted in multiple ways. While it is material (solid), it is, as I've suggested so far, processual: changing, open-ended, oriented to the future. If, following Dworkin, media are not objects, they might be considered *things*. Indeed, for Celia Lury (2004; see also Lash and Lury 2005), contemporary media/tion works through the thingification of media, and the mediation of things – that is, processes whereby media culture involves both and things or spaces being turned into media. Hence *Trainspotting*, one of Lury's case studies, is not only a novel and film but a series of branded things, including a much-circulated and imitated poster that mediated popular culture and everyday spaces. In this way, there is a blurring of the boundaries between materiality and media.

Marc Steinberg takes up this symbiotic process in a discussion of ubiquitous media. Working with an expansive version of media, as demonstrated in the epigraph, his focus is on the Japanese animated (or anime) TV series, *Tetsuwan Atomu*, popular in the 1960s. Steinberg argues that central to the programme's success was a sticker campaign, launched in 1963 to promote Marble Chocolate, a once market-leader chocolate aimed at children, whose sales had declined because of rival brands. The stickers featured the main character, Atomu, from the TV series in various energetic moves (running, flying, boxing).[2] Steinberg approaches the stickers as a 'thingified image' (2009: 116). However, he argues that,

---

2 An important aspect of Steinberg's argument, not covered here due to space, is concerned with character merchandising.

even as the stickers communicated with the manga and the anime, they also had a material specificity of their own which was the ... perhaps most important, reason for their success. This specificity had three components to it. First, the *mobility* of the stickers; they were small, highly portable, and came included in the relatively affordable Meiji candy. Second, their adhesiveness or *stickerability*; the stickers could be placed anywhere, and attached to any surface. And finally, following from the first two aspects, they could be *seen anytime*. (2009: 122)

This '*any movement, anywhere, anytime*' (2009: 122) capacity of the stickers is what defines them as ubiquitous media. Important again here is the blurring between media and materiality – indeed, the 'material specificity' of the stickers – their size and ease of movement, their stickerability and their capacity to be seen anytime – feeds into their workings as media/tion. As Mike Featherstone puts it in defining what ubiquitous media refers to, 'media are now differentiated, dispersed and multi-modal' (2009: 2). Media and materials are movement.

Sarah Kember and Joanna Zylinska's (2012) work on life and/after new media, and specifically the distinction they draw between media and mediation, which they posit in terms of temporality, is instructive on this point.[3] Kember and Zylinksa understand media/tion in terms of its vitality or 'lifeness', which they explain as 'the possibility of the emergence of forms always new, or its potentiality to generate unprecedented connections and unexpected events' (2012: xvii). They define this processual and transformative quality as *mediation*, where 'mediation is the orginary process of media emergence, with media being seen as (ongoing) stabilisations of the media flow' (2012: 21). In other words, mediation is the flow out of which media are 'temporary fixings' (2012: 21). These relations between mediation and media are suggestive for a further understanding of glitter as thing. In the first instance, it is through the perpetual movement of mediation that media are created. Second, Kember and Zylinska argue that 'in that process of ongoing mediation, with its inevitable ebbs and flows, singular stabilisations, fixes, or cuts to this process *matter*' (2012: 22): if 'matter' is taken to refer both to that which comes to

---

3 Although they also make a distinction between their argument on mediation and Lash and Lury's (2012: 22–23).

be important or significant and to 'substance' or 'material', the temporary firmings-up of mediation as media are 'things' in the sense that they are both media and material. Third, the communicative quality of media is of interest here, which Kember and Zylinska elucidate as 'more than facilitation of a dialog or discourse between two human entities. Media "communicate" in the sense of *always remaining turned toward what is not them'* (2012: 21). The fixing of media out of the flow of mediation is but one of the possibilities of media, in that media may (have been) fixed otherwise or differently. The 'communicative aspect' (2012: 21) of media thus gestures towards the 'being and becoming' of media. Both media and mediation are future-oriented.

The discussion of media and mediation so far all feed into my understanding of glitter as thing, and in particular the points they raise regarding ubiquity, movement and transformation. I draw on these different, although resonant, senses of media and mediation throughout the book as they become significant to the interdisciplinary scholarly imagination developed (see Introduction). To these versions of media and mediation, I add two further senses of the terms. The first, which is discussed in more detail in Chapter 2, is that of a 'mediator', a concept drawn from Deleuze's work on fabulation that sees people and things as mediators of the creation of new worlds. Mediators here are the material and immaterial processes via which glimpses of, embodiments of and/or actualisations of new worlds are made possible. The second concerns an understanding of a thing as material and affective, highlighting the importance of becoming, that is, the capacity of things to work across and indeed perhaps confuse or diffuse the boundaries between humans and non-humans. As a thing, glitter has the capacity to create affects in bodies, making it difficult to draw clear lines between the body and the thing. Indeed, as I have argued previously (Coleman 2009; 2012, 2018b), seemingly distinct entities made of different 'stuff' – such as mass-media images and human bodies – become through their affective relations (see also Paasonen 2011). Such an understanding sees media as necessarily material, in that it is felt, embodied and lived out, and materiality as necessarily mediated, in that materiality is constituted through the immateriality of images and imagination. It also draws attention to the transformative capacities of affective relations; becoming is an ongoing process.

Following the Thing II: Attentiveness, Affect, Communication

A methodology of following the lifeness and liveliness of a thing that is in constant movement and an emergent relationality 'means the investigator must descend into the world with the objects and be on the move with them' (Lash and Lury 2005: 29). As things, materials/media (such as glitter) are not so much texts to be interpreted; rather, 'corresponding to the shift from texts to objects is a shift in how we encounter culture: from reading and interpretation to perception, experience and operationality' (Lash and Lury 2005: 29). Following the thing therefore involves not so much a concern with symbolism and signification, but more with process, transformation, embodiment and affect (see Lash and Lury 2005: 29; Coleman 2009, 2012). Put slightly differently, media are affective and embodied, and communication is that which occurs not only through symbolism but also materially. Working with models of signification to understand glitter as thing may not, then, grasp what it does to particular bodies.

Feminist new materialisms, which focus on the potential vitality of matter, are helpful for developing these arguments further. In her influential account of the vibrancy of matter, Jane Bennett (2010) also describes her methodology in terms of 'following', suggesting that,

> there is ... public value in following the scent of a nonhuman, thingly power, the material agency of natural bodies and technological artifacts. Here I mean 'to follow' in the sense in which Jacques Derrida develops it in the context of his mediation on animals. Derrida points to the intimacy between being and following: to be (anything, anyone) is always to be following (something, someone), always to be in response to call from something, however nonhuman it may be. (2010: xiii)

In pointing to the intimacy between the follower and followed, Bennett draws attention to the affectivity between things and humans – the capacity of things to affect as well as be affected. As noted above, and in resonance with Lash and Lury's methodology, to understand things as affective is to realign the hierarchy between humans and non-humans so that these things are on the same plane, albeit with different capacities (for example, humans having the capacity for intentionality and reflection).

Such a methodology is in part an attempt to notice and attend to the often overlooked participation of things in the world/worldings. In a discussion of the new materialisms, art practices and research, Barbara Bolt argues that the 'materiality of matter lies at the core of creative practice' and that '[t]he material facts of artistic practice appear so self-evident and integral to our understanding of art that it might seem unremarkable to frame them in terms of the material turn' (2012: 5). For Bolt, 'materials' refer to a wide range of 'bodies that enable art to come into being – the material bodies of artists and theorists, the matter of the medium, the technologies of production and the immaterial bodies of knowledge that form discourse around art' (2012: 7). While Bolt's focus is on artistic practice, her suggestion that materials participate in – indeed, are core to – how art emerges can be seen as having implications for a methodology of following the thing. Glitter is a ubiquitous thing that connects, assembles and intra-acts (Barad 2007) with other things, including furniture and floors, suitcases and bags, and human bodies, and sets off a series of affects including pleasure and enchantment, irritation and frustration. Moreover, following glitter enables a book to emerge that brings together a disparate range of worlds that are connected through following glitter but that might not otherwise have been brought into the same space/time. Through following glitter, the book emerges as an assemblage where collaging and waste, vagazzling, glitter-bombing and filmic conventions are understood as in relations: distinct and connected, diverse and multiple and with similarities.

Methodology, Collaboration, Ethics, Politics

To return to Bennett's explanation of being 'struck' by – affected by – things, discussed above, her approach can be seen to reinforce the primacy of the human in that things produced affects 'in her'. In some ways this is unavoidable; it is impossible to slough off humanness and become thing – and, from a feminist position, it is also undesirable, as one consequence of such a move is to relieve oneself of the responsibilities and accountabilities of humanness (see also Barad 2007; Suchman

2007).[4] In dialogue with such potential problems, Bennett discusses the importance of understanding politics as affective in her work from *The Enchantment of Modern Life* (2001) to *Vibrant Matter* (2010), and explains that her aim is,

to focus less on the enhancement to human relational capacities resulting from affective catalysts and more on the catalyst itself as it exists in nonhuman bodies. This power is not transpersonal or intersubjective but impersonal, an affect intrinsic to forms that cannot be imagined (even ideally) as persons. I now empha-sise even more how the figure of enchantment points in two directions: the first toward the humans who *feel* enchanted and whose agentic capacities may be thereby strengthened, and the second toward the agency of the things that *pro-duce* (helpful, harmful) effects in human and other bodies. Organic and inorganic, natural and cultural objects (these distinctions are not particularly salient here) *all* are affective. (2010: xii)

Following vibrant things involves both accounting for the human who is affected (in this case, the researcher, me; possibly, you) *and* the things that affect. Both humans and non-humans are affective. What this suggests in terms of methodological decision-making is that things as well as humans play a role. The things are vibrant and alive. They are affective (at the least). For example, in the collaging workshops, glitter emerged as a particularly significant material out of a range of other materials. It did this in part because of its capacity to engage and occupy the girls working in the class-room with the various collaging materials. The affective relations between the girls and the glitter, then, are not uni-directional, working from the human to the material. As much as the girls chose the glitter, the glitter chose them. And, while the affectivity of glitter for these girls is captivating, not all humans are enchanted by it.

The attention that Bennett gives to things is her way of developing an understanding of agency as distributed across a wide range of matter and

4 Although, of course, 'humanness' has not been attributed or available to all humans in the same way, and those who do not meet the white, heterosexual, middle-class, able-bodied male norm are often positioned and understood in terms of thingness or objectness. For a discussion on how women's bodies are positioned as both subjects and object of visual culture, and for what an ontology of becoming might offer to such work, see Coleman (2009).

materials, both human and non-human. Such an understanding of the life/liveliness of non-human things requires a methodology capable of grasping such vibrancy and movement. If things are affective and have an autonomy that is bound up with humans but not always determined by them, Bennett asks:

What method could possibly be appropriate for the task of speaking a word for vibrant matter? How to describe without thereby erasing the independence of things? How to acknowledge the obscure but ubiquitous intensity of impersonal affect? What seems to be needed is a certain willingness to appear naïve or foolish, to affirm what Adorno called his 'clownish traits'. (2010: xiii)

The 'willingness to appear naïve or foolish' that Bennett introduces here is the beginning of the methodology that she sets out for grasping the vibrancy of things.[5] As indicated in the epigraph, Bennett argues for a 'lingering' in and with the things that fascinate. She describes this lingering in terms of 'a cultivated, patient, sensory attentiveness to nonhuman forces operating outside and inside the human body' that she explains as 'learn[ing] how to induce an attentiveness to things and their affects' (2010: xiv; see also Stewart 2007). Cultivating this kind of attentiveness, she argues, challenges the binary between active human subjects and passive objects, and enables a consideration of the materiality and affectivity of seemingly different categories of things.

Such an approach re-thinks what ethics and politics might be, in that non-humans as well as humans act and have effects in/on the world. While this does not necessarily mean that every materiality has equal power – humans 'can experience themselves as forming intentions and as standing apart from their actions to reflect on them later' (Bennett 2010: 31) – it does involve a regard for the relations between and assemblage of humans and non-humans. Because of the tradition in which the social sciences and humanities have concerned themselves with human agency, Bennett's focus is on levelling out the hierarchy between humans and non-humans; that is, the cultivation of an attention to things is an attempt to see what happens – theoretically, methodologically, analytically, politically and

5 For more specifically on foolishness and naivety when working with feminist new materialist practices, see Coleman, Page and Palmer (2019) and Coleman and Osgood (in preparation).

ethically – when things and their acts, affects and effects are taken seriously. The foolishness and naïveté that she points to in the quotation above are part of the methodology that Bennett advocates, which entails an openness to what things might do. She argues,

> For *this* task, demystification, that most popular of practices in critical theory, should be used with caution and sparingly, because demystification presumes that at the heart of any event or process lies a *human* agency that has illicitly been projected into things. This hermeneutics of suspicion calls for theorists to be on high alert for signs of the secret truth (a human will to power) below the false appearance of nonhuman agency. (2010: xiv)

The positing of critique as a 'hermeneutics of suspicion' in contrast to the possibility of positive formulations' (2010: xv) has proved problematic for some feminist theorists.[6] Kember, for example, argues that Bennett's work 'seeks a knowledge formed through direct engagement with life, through contact and openness rather than an intellectual mastery and control' (Kember 2016: 27).[7] For Kember, this approach is 'reactionary and foundationalist' (2016: 28). She argues that 'contemporary feminism in the material mode' (2016: 28) – including Bennett's – is consistent with 'masculine, male-dominated metaphysics' (2016: 28) such as object-oriented philosophy (OOP). Kember's objections to OOP are that, in positing an ontology of objects-in-themselves, OOP abandons critique for a celebratory account of objects and, in so doing, it becomes 'compatible, if not necessarily complicit with, industry goals oriented to novelty and innovation – *i*Phones[n] – rather than invention and intervention' (2016: 24). Similarly, Bennett's abandonment of critique is both based on

---

6 The term 'hermeneutics of suspicion' is most readily associated with the work of Eve Kofosky Sedgwick (2003), who argued for a theoretical approach based on 'reparative' readings instead.

7 It is important to note that in this discussion, Kember's focus is on Bennett's book, *The Enchantment of Modern Life: Attachments, Crossings, and Ethics* (2001), rather than *Vibrant Matter: A Political Ecology of Things* (2010), which I've been discussing so far in this chapter. However, Bennett's later book takes up the approach set out in the former book, not least in '[t]he idea ... that moments of sensuous enchantment with the everyday world – with nature but also with commodities and other cultural products – might augment the motivational energy needed to move selves from the endorsement of ethical principles to the actual practice of ethical behaviours' (2010: xi).

a mistaken belief that demystification is necessarily suspicious (rather than interventionist), and occurs when 'enchantment and mystification double-time as marketing and advertising strategies, as key to "a cynical world of business as usual" as well as processes of normalisation and discrimination' (reference omitted, Kember 2016: 28) – in other words, at precisely a time when demystification and suspicion is required (see also McNeil 2011). Kember goes on to argue that Bennett's affirmative and positive approach is also marked 'by a tendency to reassert rather than reinvent nature' (2016: 28).

Kember's critique of 'contemporary feminism in a material mode' is an important reminder about the necessity for critical theories to remain sensitive to what is at stake in any account, be that the specifics of the things analysed and/or the historical moment at which the analysis is performed. For this book, this involves being attentive to how glitter is often marketed and advertised as 'enchanting and mystical' in ways that involve 'processes of normalisation and discrimination', including the reassertion and remaking of gendered, heterosexual, raced, classed and aged relations of power. What I take from Bennett's development of 'a cultivated, patient, sensory attentiveness to nonhuman forces' for a study of the future politics of glitter is its attempt to grasp what it is about some things that seems to make them especially affective in some worlds/worldings.

The methodology of following glitter, then, and the assemblage it produces is necessarily partial and situated. This is so because there are many routes along which glitter, as a ubiquitous thing, can be followed; as Caroline Knowles puts it in setting out her methodology for following the global paths of flip-flops, '[a]t all points the trail splintered and moved off in many directions. I could only follow one of them. Thus even in following a single object there are unaccountable potential trails to take into account' (2014: 16). Knowles' comments here point both to the 'unaccountable potential trails' that do not become part of a research project (the virtuality surrounding the actual, or what Karen Barad (2007) might term the boundary-making cuts that are necessary to make a research project manageable and accountable) and to methodological decisions regarding how a thing is followed along a particular route out of many potential ones.

Traditionally, a sociological account would emphasise the human researcher as the sole or primary agent in making decisions. However, the methodology of following the thing that I am putting together here emphasises not only the agency of humans (me, the people who engage in different ways with glitter) but also of materials/media (things). That is, as a thing, glitter itself has agency – is alive, animated – and participates in methodological decision-making. As I, human researcher, selected tubes of glitter to include in the range of materials for the girls to potentially work with, the glitter selected me to notice it (see also Despret 2004). It had a particular vibrancy that forced me to follow its distributed agency.

A methodology of following the thing is necessarily partial and situated, then, because it involves following glitter to some places and not others. It is also partial and situated because it responds to the specificity of the followed and the follower. In her work on art, and specifically painting, Katve-Kaisa Kontturi argues that following is a mode of collaboration between humans and non-humans. Drawing on Brian Massumi's (1992) description of how a woodworker 'must follow the grain of the wood, to work *with* it', she argues:

it is a painter's task to follow the qualities of paint. And whereas it is the woodworker's job to bring the qualities of wood to a certain expression, such as a table, the painter faces perhaps even more challenging a task: she must collaborate with the paint (and other materials) to create something new. What the woodworker and the painter have in common is that it is not simply their intention or will that defines the process, the creation. Instead, creation necessitates collaboration with and not a mastery over the material. This is when 'a [wo]man discovers rhythm as matter and material' and where 'it is no longer inner vision ... but manual power' that directs the process. (Deleuze 2003: 108, in Kontturi 2018: 110)

In Kontturi's terms, this book may be understood as a collaboration between myself and glitter, in that it follows glitter in ways that create a project that is not complete, unified or finished – I do not gain mastery over glitter – but rather an assemblage of cases and examples that for me are vibrant. Again, this is in some ways unavoidable. Research projects and the books and other outputs associated with them often (usually?) consist of the researcher following an interest that is affectively elicited in them through their emergent relations with things. However, this is not often (usually?) remarked upon. In developing the cultivated attention to the affectivity of things, it is crucial to note this point. It is also crucial, as I have suggested, to see this cultivated attention as generated, in part as least, through and to the affectivity of things; as I noted above, the things have vibrancy and 'strike' me/the researcher.

Indeed, my account of noticing the glitter in the collaging workshops, or, perhaps, slightly earlier when purchasing the materials for the workshops, is itself partial and yet not quite situated. It has the not-quite-right effect of marking a beginning of the vibrancy of glitter and setting up a logical route to the writing and publication of this book. Instead, this noticing of glitter might better be understood as 'in the middle', or *in media res*, as Lury (2012) puts it. The chapter on collaging is placed, deliberately, in 'the middle' of the book, at the juncture between the more theoretically and methodologically oriented discussion, and the more empirically oriented focus of the following chapters. Indeed, as Lury points out, a 'middle position is one in which, while the (critical) subject is always in relation to an (epistemic) object, this is a relation that is never stable, is always continually re-established. This might be described as a situation of perpetual animation' (2012: 192). Placing the chapter where I seemingly initially noticed glitter 'in the middle' seeks to dislodge a simple origin story and indicate instead the ways in which following glitter spreads out rhizomatically to the histories of glitter, different accounts of politics, media and materials, and to different practices that in various ways involve glitter. As such, 'the middle' is not necessarily to be found at the half-way point from the beginning and the end, but rather is some-where in-between, in the process of becoming.

The *Futures* of Following the Thing

Following the 'thing' is my way of drawing together different literatures on objects, materials and media to emphasise their common concerns with perpetual movement and transformation. This is not an abstract exercise but rather a methodology developed to understand some of the specific qualities of glitter. Glitter in the terms that I understand and explore it in this book is a material, a medium, a commodity. Glitter is ubiquitous. It moves, and spreads. It stays and it sticks. It is affective and vibrant. It changes and transforms. Indeed, my understanding of glitter as transformational is key to the methodology of following the thing. In addition to this methodology being partial and situated because it responds to the specific relations between a followed and follower, it is also partial and situated because the what, who and how involved in the following have lives and livelinesses that change and transform beyond, after or in excess of what is captured in a particular project. Put another way, glitter not only worlds in ways other than those discussed in this book, but the worldings at stake here are still continuing, now and into various futures – most obviously as waste, for example.

Following, as I understand it, is open-ended, future-oriented. I follow glitter *across* different worlds – those of artistic and embodied practices, filmic conventions, activism, natural environments – and in the *making* of different worlds. To follow glitter, then, is to be attentive to its becoming, its worldings. As Kontturi notes, '[f]ollowing aims at being confluent with the present always on the verge of opening into the future. To follow is to become with' (2018: 13). To follow glitter is also to be attentive to the ways these worldings are themselves processes that are unfinished, are in the middle. These worldings might go on to open into other futures, which may not be straightforwardly evident but may be scattered and sticky, nonlinear and intensive. This following, I argue, is political in that the making of new futures might and might not shore up existing power relations, might and might not create alternatives to what exists in the present. The task of following glitter, therefore, is to cultivate awareness of what futures glitter makes, and how.

Positing following as a methodology as well as a theory is intended to make explicit how the book is partial and situated in various ways, as discussed, and to provide a rationale for how and why specific worlds are drawn together in this book. I move between discussions of workshops where glitter was provided as a material to work with, and analyses of instances where glitter is part of everyday mediated lives. While the focus on workshops is most explicitly 'methodological', in that the workshops are a method of working with glitter, I understand following more broadly as a method; following is a means of explaining the assemblage of glitterworlds in the book. Rather than follow a specific type of glitter from its production along supply chains and to its consumption and life as waste, for instance, or focus exclusively on glitter as it appears and is used in a particular industry or sphere of everyday life (as make-up, or in nurseries, or by boat manufacturers), I instead follow glitter as it traverses and makes different worlds. This draws attention both to the qualities of glitter to disperse and to the ubiquity of glitter in contemporary everyday life. It contextualises the instances out of many where glitter 'struck' me. It also seeks to capture – temporarily and incompletely – just how glitter is always potentially opening into other futures.

2

The Future Politics of Glitter: Plastic Hopes and Fears

Glitter is not just annoying, it could be bad for the environment. (Willingham 2017, CNN)

[M]ore than a substance, plastic is the very idea of its infinite transformation; as its everyday name indicates, it is ubiquity made visible. And it is this, in fact, which makes it a miraculous substance. (Barthes 2009: 97)

Plastic is 'nothing if not oriented to the future.' (Gabrys, Hawkins and Michael 2013b: 6)

Glitter has recently attracted a good deal of alarm and reporting in the mass media due to concern about microbeads and calls for and implementation of bans on them. Microbeads are tiny pieces of plastic, less than 0.5mm in length, added to everyday products including facewash, cosmetics, toothpaste and abrasive cleaners, that are made of polyethylene or other petrochemicals such as polypropylene and polystyrene. Their size mean they easily move into water filtration systems and onwards into the sea and food chain, and fish and birds more generally (Thorogood 2016). While glitter is a microplastic rather than a microbead, similar debates have arisen around it, and calls for it to be banned have been made by scientists, environmentalists and early childhood workers, as the headline from CNN above, and these headlines from articles from BBC 3 online and the *Guardian*, respectively, show:

Should glitter be banned? Scientists say glitter is bad for the environment, so should we stop using it altogether? (Cashin 2017)

Nurseries ban glitter in pre-Christmas drive for cleaner seas. (Harvey 2017)

To understand its materiality and its politics, then, it is necessary to locate glitter within a wider context of plastic.[1]

In this chapter, I outline the understanding of politics that this book works with to explore glitter and glitterworld(ing)s, emphasising in particular the importance of futures in these politics. As I set out in the Introduction, glitterworlds are always in the process of worlding, and as Jennifer Gabrys, Gay Hawkins and Mike Michael note in the epigraph to the chapter, as a plastic, glitter is itself future-oriented. In the first part of the chapter, I take up the concerns and calls for bans on glitter in order to consider the dominant way in which the politics of plastic is framed today. As waste, plastic is generally understood as having a limited lifespan, after which it is discarded and becomes an environmental problem. While not disputing the politics that emerge from an understanding of plastic-as-waste, I aim to demonstrate that a plurality of politics exist alongside this particular version. I explore how a politics organised around an understanding of plastic-as-waste operates according to a future that is imagined in terms of fear – an affect that is at odds with the more celebratory and joyful accounts that permeate how glitter is marketed and experienced by many people, where glitter is framed as hopeful, or, as Roland Barthes puts it above, as transformational and (potentially) miraculous. A politics of glitter, then, must be able to account for a future that is both fearful *and* hopeful.

I expand on this approach to the politics of glitter in the second half of the chapter, which introduces some of the key concepts that are developed in later chapters as I follow glitter and its worldings: hope, fabulation and pre-figurative politics. While these concepts, as I discuss them here, have different theoretical trajectories and emerge in relation to specific political, ethical and philosophical concerns, what cuts across them is an interest in the creation of different, and better, futures and an appreciation of how this future is anticipated in the present. In working

1 I do not include a history of plastic here. For this, see, for example, Sparke (1994), Meikle (1995), Shove, Watson, Hand and Ingram (2007) and Gabrys, Hawkins and Michael (2013b). For an account of the journeys that one global plastic object, the flip-flop, takes, see Knowles (2014). I also do not comment on the work on plasticity by a number of theorists and philosophers, including Malabou (2005) and Papadopoulos (2011), although there are resonances between them and the work on plastics I do discuss.

with these concepts, then, I aim to complicate a linear model of time, where the future emerges predictably out of the present and past, and instead outline an understanding of time as multiple and diverse. While the future is that which is not yet here, it is also that which is folded into the present. This understanding of time raises important questions for politics regarding how the future is both separate to and yet part of the present, and thus it requires us to attend to the practices – imaginative and material – through which the ubiquity of glitter is involved in worldings.

Plastic Imaginaries: Ubiquity, Movement, Politics

According to a number of popular histories (see, for example, Hibou 2011; Oyler 2015; Stoddard 2017), modern glitter was invented in 1934 in America by a machinist, Henry Ruschmann, who discovered a way to cut and grind up plastic or mylar sheets (a specific type of plastic sheet made from the resin of polyethylene terephthalate (PET)) into tiny pieces. Meadowbrook Inventions – the company founded by Ruschmann and based in New Jersey – describes glitter as 'precision-cut speciality film or foil typically produced in sizes .004 x .004" [approximately 0.1mm] or larger' (Meadowbrook Inventions 2015). A recent *New York Times* article, titled 'What is glitter?' (Weaver 2018), goes inside the Glitterex factory, also based in New Jersey, to detail the complexity of producing glitter and the secrecy that its clients demand of the production process. The founder of the company, Babu Shetty, explains that at Glitterex, glitter begins with polyester film, known as mylar, which is then metalised on both sides with aluminium. The rainbow colours of glitter can be produced in one of two ways. First, holographic glitter involves 'embossing a fine pattern onto film, so that the surface reflects light in different directions' (Weaver 2018) and, second, 'more subtle iridescent glitter' is made from 233 layers of clear film, 'composed of polymers with different refractive indexes' that make up the visible spectrum of colours (Weaver 2018). According to Sheppey, '[e]ach layer is half the wavelength of light' (Weaver 2018) and the glitter shimmers by changing colour as it catches the light at different degrees. The journalist who visited Glitterex remarks of the ubiquity of glitter:

It's impossible to recreate the light-catching effect of glitter without using tiny particles of something, which means that if an object looks glittery upon close inspection (a credit card design; an N.F.L. helmet; a jet ski paint job), there are good odds that it contains glitter. Researchers and zookeepers sometimes mix glitter with animal feed to track animals (polar bears; elephants; domestic cats) via sparkly feces. Plywood manufacturers insert hidden layers of colored glitter in their products to prevent counterfeiting. Because glitter is difficult to remove completely from an area into which it has been introduced, and because individual varieties can be distinguished under a microscope, it can serve as useful crime scene evidence; years ago the F.B.I. contacted Glitterex to catalog samples of its products. The average American, said Mr. Shetty, sees glitter every day. Most of it is hexagonal. (Weaver 2018)

Meadowbrook also describe the ubiquity of glitter today, noting that the company produces glitter in different sizes that is put to many different uses, as discussed in the Introduction. The story of glitter as invented by Ruschmann posits its origin as a 'discovery' and emphasises the (male) human inventor. In so doing, it perpetuates the 'great man' version of history (see, e.g., Kelly 1984; Scott 1988) and neglects how invention is a socio-technical process involving many different human and non-human actors (see, e.g., Barry 2005). It also sets into chain a seemingly inevitable expansion of glitter where its 'applications are limitless' and it is used 'across the globe'.

However, discussing the so-called 'Plastic Age' of the twentieth century, Bernadette Bensaude Vincent (2013) argues that '[p]lastics are more than just ubiquitous manufactured products that are used all over the world. As plastics began to spread in the daily experience of billions of people, new concepts of design were developed that reshaped our view of nature and technology' (2013: 17). In other words, Bensaude Vincent seeks to account for the material-technical-socio-cultural entanglements that the spread of plastics was involved in, discussing the complexity of some of the processes by which the material of plastic and its potential use in different contexts took hold. For example, the versatility of plastic was initially viewed by consumers as a 'major imperfection', as a material having a single function – a glass for red wine as opposed to a glass for white wine as opposed to a glass for champagne – 'was seen as a mark of superiority' (2013: 19). The versatility or plasticity of plastic was seen as 'the hallmark of cheap substitutes, forever doomed to imitate more authentic, natural materials' (2013: 19). Similarly, its impermanence and superficiality also generated misgivings. Today, however, partly due to marketing and promotional campaigns, another version of plastic also exists where they 'are no longer considered cheap substitutes. They are praised because they can be moulded easily into a large variety of forms and remain relatively stable in their manufactured form' (Bensaude Vincent 2013: 19).

In his brief remarks on plastic, Barthes also comments on this 'evolution in the myth of "imitation" materials', noting how until the mid-1950s when he was writing, imitation materials were deemed pretentious and/or superficial. What plastic achieves, however, is not imitation so much as ubiquity and use. Barthes argues that plastic is not so concerned with 'reproducing cheaply' more luxurious materials, but rather has 'climbed down' and is now a 'prosaic', 'common', 'household' material (1957/2009: 98). As an artificial material, plastic aims not to 'regain or imitate' natural materials (as 'the myth of "imitation" materials' would suggest) but rather its very artificiality provides a 'triumphant reason for its existence', as it gives rise to the invention of new forms and uses, and even to the possibility of 'objects be[ing] invented for the sole pleasure of using them' (2009: 98–99).

Barthes' comments were written following a visit to a trade show of plastic, which showed the process by which 'raw telluric matter' was made, via a machine 'hardly watched over by an attendant in a cloth cap, half-god, half-robot', into finished objects (2009: 97). Barthes was, as he puts it, 'witness [to] the accomplishment of the magical operation par excellence: the transmutation of matter' (2009: 97). The ease with which plastic lends itself to transmutation into a plethora of 'terminal forms' – 'suitcase, brush, car-body, toy, fabric, tube, basin or paper' (2009: 97) – leads him to describe plastic, as noted in the epigraph, as a 'miraculous substance'. He goes on to say, 'a miracle is always a sudden transformation of nature. Plastic remains impregnated throughout with this wonder: *it is less a thing than the trace of a movement*' (2009: 97, my emphasis). This formulation of plastic as 'the trace of a movement' highlights the malleability of plastic, where transformation refers not only to how various forms are made from raw materials, but also to how technological, socio-cultural and natural relations are refigured through plastic. It also, I suggest, gestures towards the future-orientation of plastic; movement and transformation indicate that plastics are open-ended, in process, becoming.

It is also worth noting the more general tone with which Barthes describes and explains plastic, which is one of wonder. Plastic, as a novel and prosaic material, is miraculous, triumphant: 'the whole world can be plasticised', he notes (2009: 99). Barthes' comments, then, can be understood in terms of a more general utopianism ascribed to plastic in the mid- to late twentieth century. Jeffrey L. Meikle (1995) traces the role of plastic in American culture, arguing that in the 1920s and 1930s, it was seen as encompassing a 'utopian potential as a substance capable of transforming the material conditions that had always limited human life' (1995: 67). The Plastic Age 'offered humanity an opportunity to gain freedom from chance and from nature's imperfections' (1995: 68, see also Clarke 1999 on the links between Tupperware and utopia). However, Meikle (1997) also describes how the celebration of plastic was coupled with criticisms of it, which ranged from fears about a loss of control over nature, to concern over pollution, to condemnation of consumerism and the artificiality of everyday life. These contradictory understandings of plastic co-exist; Meikle points out that '[p]otential for this vague fear of plastic extended back to the 1920s when publicists celebrated new synthetic materials as magic products of alchemical wizardry rather than of rational chemical processes', thereby 'encourag[ing] ignorance' in ordinary citizens about the production of plastic and producing a feeling that 'the forces of nature' were becoming untamed (1997: 280).

What might these understandings of plastic have to offer the approach to glitter taken in this book? First, 'more than just ubiquitous manufactured products that are used all over the world' – the 'limitless' applications that Meadowbrook Inventions point to – the specific relations between technology, nature and culture that glitter is involved in might be examined. For example, the concerns about the environmental impacts of glitter outlined above demonstrate anxiety about the difficulty of making and maintaining firm boundaries between culture and nature, as cultural products leak into nature. If glitter is understood within a history of plastics, it is possible to see how hopes and fears regarding what it might do and where it might go accompany each other. Thus, contemporary concern about the damage to the environment that glitter is causing is part of a long-running set of reservations regarding 'alchemical wizardry' (Meikle 1997: 280) and the current celebration of glitter as fun and glamourous extends the attitudes and experiences of plastic as miraculous.

Second, and relatedly, the values associated with plastic – 'lightness, superficiality, versatility and impermanence' (Bensaude Vincent 2013: 18) – and how understandings or valuations of these values change, are also of relevance to glitter. The versatility of glitter is highlighted by Meadowbrook Inventions; glitter is valued in a range of industries and activities, and can be put to multiple uses within these, demonstrating that its adaptability and flexibility is prized. The values of lightness and superficiality also speak to the materiality of glitter, albeit in not quite the same ways that they do to plastic more generally. Whereas lightness for plastic is connected to its weight (or lack of it compared, for example, to wood or metal), as noted above, one of the main attributes of glitter is its sparkle, which is produced through its ability to reflect light. The superficiality of plastic is, according to Bensaude Vincent, because of its relative cheapness and its association with 'low', 'throwaway' cultural activities and products (theme parks, fast food, decorations...). Cultural judgements concerning superficiality are certainly evident in assessments of glitter, where they are often aged, classed and gendered. Despite its movement from being a material for children to play with to one with which adults can decorate themselves (and perhaps others – see Chapters 4 and 6), glitter remains associated with childish, irresponsible and feminised behaviour. For example, a video that accompanies the story, 'Glitter should be banned over environmental impacts, scientists warn' (Gabbatiss 2017) in the UK newspaper the *Independent*, is compiled solely of images of gold glitter make-up, a white man sprinkling purple glitter at a parade or protest (read: queer man at Gay Pride), and white women wearing glitter as face make-up and hair decoration. As I argue in more detail in the following chapters, the association between superficiality and marginality (involving femininity, class, race, youth and sexuality) is a prevalent way in which the politics of glitter as waste and/ or damaging are expressed.

As Gabrys, Hawkins and Michael point out, then, 'plastic is wrapped up in a panoply of expectations, hopes, fears and hypes' (2013b: 6).

Plastic generates hope and fears for the future, and 'instantiate the contradictions of a society oriented towards the mass manufacture of more and more disposable products' (Bensaude Vincent 2013: 24). Today, what dominate, as the headlines with which I opened the chapter suggest, are fears about how plastic generate huge amounts of waste, much of which is unable to be recycled and thus contributes to landfill and the pollution of the environments in which humans, animals and other life forms exist and endure. Once a plastic object has fulfilled its use, it is discarded and becomes waste. In terms of glitter, especially in cases where it is used for 'novelty' or 'superficial' activities, such as on greeting cards, fashion, make-up and celebrations and parades, glitter is thus a wasteful material.

Calls for a ban on glitter both emerge from and generate a politics that is both difficult and undesirable to disagree with. A contemporary understanding of the politics of glitter must take into account the effects that it has on the environment in its production (the use of the finite natural resource of oil to make plastic; see Marriott and Minio-Paluello 2013) and once it is discarded. However, a politics of glitter, or plastic more generally, must also be capable of grasping the many other politics that it might be involved in. Just as plastic gestures towards and produces a 'panoply of expectations, hopes, fears and hypes', so too does glitter. It is seen as celebratory *and* damaging, frivolous *and* deadly, decorative *and* violent. It is insubstantial and yet can have lasting, destructive affects/effects. Glitter is multiple.

Third, glitter is a thing that is future-oriented. Put another way, glitter is in the process of materialising. Third, then, as discussed above, to attend to the politics of a material that is processual, materialising, requires an openness to both what constitutes 'politics' and to how that material becomes political at specific points and in specific ways. That is, it is not always possible to know the politics of glitter in advance of its materialisation. In the rest of this chapter, I lay out the framework of politics that I work with in the book, which, put simply, understands the politics of glitter as multiple, emergent and future-oriented. This argument, as I expand on below, is not intended to dislodge or dispute the necessity for more just, respectful and careful relations between humans and environments. Rather, it is an attempt to consider what happens if the hopes that plastic once embodied, and still do embody in many instances, are taken seriously and thus to explore the 'panoply' of futures that glitter might be involved in imagining and materialising. This is not to argue that glitter is not harmful in many if not most contexts; instead it is to consider how, in sometimes mundane and small ways, glitter is *also* involved in worldings that seek to bring about a better world, albeit in ways that might not be deemed successful.

The Future Politics of Plastic

To begin to develop this framework of the politics of glitter, I want to unpack further the significance of 'the future', beginning with how understandings of plastic-as-waste(ful) are organised around images of a dystopian future. Plastic is seen as contributing to the demise of the planet. These arguments are both urgent and important; this book does not deny or repudiate them. But the project this book proposes is that it is necessary to consider the array of futures, and future politics that glitter might generate, exploring how glitter as a plastic does not always easily fit into arguments that centre on fear and dystopian futures. At the same time that dystopian futures exist as possible or plausible, the utopianism with which plastic was greeted and the positive affects that glitter may evoke are also evident.

Taking seriously the suggestion that the future politics of plastic are multiple and potentially contradictory indicates a need to consider temporality as multi-faceted and changing, non-linear and transformative. In a discussion of plastic water bottles, Gay Hawkins (2013) develops a topological account of time, which sees time not as that which proceeds linearly and progressively (from point A – the past – to point B – the present – to point C – the future), but rather as bending, curving and folding, so that the past and future may crumple with or as the present (Serres and Latour 1995; Lury, Parisi and Terranova 2012; Michael and Rosengarten 2012). Hawkins' topological approach therefore disrupts a linear understanding of the life of a plastic water bottle as useful and *then* waste by 'see[ing] how the anticipated future of the single-use PET bottle is folded into the present' (2013: 51). She argues that the disposability of plastic – its impermanence in terms of use value – is often immanent to it. A plastic water bottle made of PET, for example, 'appears as rubbish from the beginning. It may have momentary functionality as packaging or as a container, but this is generally subsumed by its more substantial material presence as a transitional object – as something that is *made to be wasted*' (2013: 50). Here, then, 'the afterlife of the bottle' – its life as waste – is 'anticipated before exchange, connecting the value of convenience to the ease with which the bottle is discarded' (2013: 51). In other words, the future of the bottle as waste is part of how its life before it is waste is defined, in terms of its design and consumption as something to be used once and discarded.

In these ways, like the single-use PET water bottle, glitter is 'a transitional object'. Its various lives are both folded into and unfold from its materiality. However, while the impermanence is a characteristic of PET bottle (they are 'made to be wasted'), the *permanence* of glitter is often remarked upon. For example, searching definitions of glitter online inevitably brings me to the following explanation, this one included on the website Urban Dicitionary (Figure 2.1):

glitter

glitter is the herpes of craft supplies
    The thing about glitter is if you have it on you be prepared to have it on you forever, cause glitter doesn't go away.
    #glitter #flare #up #dance #sand #super busy hospital 2
    by Jadykinzz October 22, 2007[2]

This capacity of glitter to never go away is also commented on in a *Guardian* column on 'the festival look' of glitter swimwear ('The latest summer trend [that] involves applying glitter directly to the skin in a swimsuit shape') has the headline, 'Glitter swimwear: you won't wear all of it for long, but you'll wear some of it for ever' (Pass Notes 2018b). And, it is at the heart of the original product, The OG Glitter Bomb, from the Ship Your Enemies Glitter website, which, accompanying a cartoon drawing of a man, dressed in a suit, opening an envelope filled with glitter, describes the bomb in terms that emphasise the capacity of glitter to last 'for weeks':

2 www.urbandictionary.com/define.php?term=Glitter, last accessed 9 August 2018.

Pay us your money provide an address anywhere in the world & we'll send your recipient so much glitter in an envelope that they'll be finding it everywhere for weeks. We'll also include a note telling the person exactly why they're receiving this terrible gift. Hint: the glitter will be mixed in with the note thus increasing maximum spillage.[3]

Adapting the topological approach advocated by Hawkins, while the impermanence (its afterlife as waste) of the PET bottle is folded into its present, it may be that the *permanence* of glitter is part of its present life. That is, the 'anticipated future' of glitter – its permanence – is always already folded into its present. Its impermanence and permanence exist together. As plastic, glitter is waste, and hence impermanent, and as a material/isation that lasts after its use, glitter is also permanent. Glitter does not always go or remain where it is intended to – it gets everywhere – but it will last.

Such an approach complicates a politics that is organised around understanding plastic as predominantly or most importantly waste, and arguing for a ban on it. While an end to plastic is not necessarily precluded from such an approach – indeed it may emerge as key to it – according to Gabrys, Hawkins and Michael, a politics that centres the materiality/ies of plastic treats plastic as an empirical problem. Taking the various but specific lives of plastic seriously – the particular contexts in which it dwells, routes that it takes and how it is used and experienced – raises questions as well as demands answers. For example, Gabrys, Hawkins and Michael ask:

What is plastic doing in the world? What might it do? Questions about the concrete effects of specific manifestations of plastics quickly lead to political entanglements, but the political questions that emerge in this study do not just stem from a human assessment of 'bad impacts'. Instead, we suggest that plastics generate a series of causes or political reverberations that genuinely constitute modes of material politics, when emerge from the concrete events of plastics in the world. The material politics of plastics can then be seen as emergent and contingent, where plastics set in motion relations between things that become sites of responsibility and effect. From this perspective, a material politics informed by plastics is less oriented toward asserting that materials are always already

3 Website last accessed 29 September 2016.

political. Instead [it] variously focus[es] on when and how plastics as materials *become* political. Through which material processes and entanglements do plastics 'force thought' and give shape to political concerns (Stengers 2010)? (2013b: 4–5)

As is indicated in this framing of a material politics of plastic, the questions (and answers) that plastic might pose are directed towards not only what plastic 'is' – its material properties – but also its unfolding and hence diverse and specific future instantiations and affects/effects – its materialisation. Plastics *become* – they are lively and have lives (see Chapter 1) – and through this becoming generate political concerns. Indeed, one of the questions that plastic generates is how to identify it as such. Max Liboiron (2016), who monitors the ingestion of plastic in fish, observes that current laboratory apparatus produce a certain amount of ambiguity about whether or not a substance found in a fish is actually plastic (see *Identifying* intervention at the end of the book). In this case, the movement of plastic creates a new set of entangled political questions concerning not only how and where it moves and what its effects are, but also what it is and how it might be identified. According to this account of plastic, the task for this book is to consider the specific and concrete ways in which glitter becomes political, which might involve its effects on the 'natural' environment in different ways and to different extents. As an empirical question, such a task will generate not a final take on the politics of glitter, but rather will lend itself to a plurality of politics – manifested via the 'emergent and contingent' contexts and framings through which glitter is approached – and will in all likelihood generate a series of further questions or 'reverberations'.

The way in which I approach the empirical problem of the politics of glitter is to see glitter as involved in the production of specific worlds. Glitter is involved in worldings. These worldings are, by necessity, unfinished, open-ended, future-oriented; the emphasis is on world*ings* to account for this dynamism. My focus is on the ways in which these worldings are created through the entanglement between humans and glitter (as well as other non-human agencies). My aim, then, is to consider what Alaimo (2010) calls 'trans-corporality', a term she coins to 'emphasis[e] the material interconnections of human corporeality with the more-than-human world – and at the same time, acknowledg[e] that material agency necessitates more capacious epistemologies' (2010: 2). In Chapter 1, I expanded on how I attempt to account for the material agency of glitter as well as the agency of humans through the development of the concept of 'the thing'. At this point, what is at stake is the ways in which worldings are '[p]otent ethical and political possibilities [that] emerge from the literal contact zone between human corporeality and more-than-human nature' (Alaimo 2010: 2). In particular, Alaimo's argument understands 'environment' in terms of a 'nature' that is necessarily entangled with 'culture' and/or the human and that has its own 'needs, claims and action' (2010: 2). Moreover, 'by underscoring that *trans* indicates movement across different sites, trans-corporeality also opens up a mobile space that acknowledges the often unpredictable and unwanted actions of human bodies, nonhuman creatures, ecological systems, chemical agents, and other actors' (2010: 2).

Taking up Alaimo's work, which investigates these possibilities through a focus on the 'natural' environment, is not accidental; given the discussion so far regarding the artificiality of plastic and its relationship with nature, I draw on it precisely to develop an approach that keeps in play the political questions that plastic-as-waste provoke as well as those that emerge from a more pluralistic understanding of what politics might involve, as I've discussed so far. Her emphasis on *trans*-corporeality also resonates with my exploration of glitterworlds, that is, with how glitter moves across and comes to partly constitute different sites, blurring boundaries between nature and culture and setting up contestations about the making and disturbance of boundaries that are difficult to settle. For Alaimo, this concept is therefore concerned with the potential uncertainty and open-endedness of movement – an understanding of matter that might be further expanded through the relationship between movement and transformation discussed so far. For example, for Barthes, movement involves not only travel and mobility, but also the ways in which a material might become something else (see also Chapter 1 on the movement and transformation of things). Furthermore, Alaimo points to what might be considered the development of a project similar in spirit in her account of what she understands 'matter' to refer to:

By attending to the material interconnections between the human and the more-than-human world, it may be possible to conjure an ethics lurking in an idiomatic definition of *matter* (or *the matter*): 'The condition of or state of things regarding a person or thing, esp. as a subject of concern or wonder' (*Oxford English Dictionary*). Concern and wonder converge when the context for ethics becomes not merely social but material – the emergent, ultimately unmappable landscapes of interacting biological, climatic, economic and political forces. (2010: 2)

Through a focus on material politics, concern and wonder 'converge' – or, in the terms that I have been developing so far, may co-exist and co-emerge.

Fabulation, Hope and Pre-figurative Politics

To unpack the multiple and potentially contradictory politics of glitter, and to explore further the non-linearity and diversity of temporality discussed above, it is productive to consider some theories that are concerned with what I would call future politics. In particular, the concept of fabulation, found in the work of Bergson and Deleuze and those inspired by it, is helpful in developing an understanding of the relations between the present and future and how these are both affective and political. Bergson (1977) develops fabulation as a means to account for myth-making, which he explains in terms of humans' 'virtual instinct' (1977: 110) to anthropomorphise natural phenomena, such as earthquakes and lightning, and assign intentionality to them, leading to the invention of religion, gods and other spirits.[4] John Mullarkey (2007) explains that, although for Bergson 'it connotes fabrication, fabulation is not wholly unnatural, nor unfounded: it is not *fictitious* or *purely* relative to individual whimsey' (2007: 54). Instead, fabulation is 'connected to the "paradox of fiction", to the problem of why we feel real emotions for unreal (fictitious) people and the events that befall them. The answer from Bergson is that fiction makes events (and the people involved in events) come *alive* for us, not just in make-believe, but at a very present and real (though primitive) level of perception' (2007: 54).

As fictitious and yet 'a very present and real' perception, Mullarkey argues that fabulation is a 'type of "seeing as", that is, fabulation is a

---

4 For a more detailed discussion of fabulation in Bergson's work, see Mullarkey (2007) and Bogue (2006).

representation or *mediation*' (2007: 54). Deleuze expands on Bergson's concept of fabulation, arguing that it is 'the act of telling tales' (1995: 125) – an act of creation that occurs through mediators:

Mediators are fundamental. Creation's all about mediators. Without them nothing happens. They can be people – for a philosopher, artists or scientists; for a scientist, philosophers or artists – but things too, even plants or animals, as in Castaneda. Whether they're real or imaginary, animate or inanimate, you have to form your mediators. (1995: 125)

While Bergson's focus is on fabulation as a process of myth-making through religion, spirituality and morality, Deleuze primarily develops his take on fabulation through art and artists, arguing that '[t]o catch someone in the act of telling tales is to catch the movement of constitution of a people' (1995: 125–126). Deleuze seeks to 'take up Bergson's notion of fabulation and give it a political meaning' (1995: 173), seeing the constitution of a people as a creative and political movement:

A people isn't something already there. A people, in a way, is what's missing, as Paul Klee used to say. Was there ever a Palestinian people? Israel says no. Of course there was, but that's not the point. The thing is, once the Palestinians have been thrown out of their territory, then to the extent that they resist they enter the process of constituting a people. ... So, to the established fictions that are always rooted in a colonist's discourse, we oppose a minority discourse, with mediators. (1995: 126)

Deleuze here links mediation, creation and politics, arguing that fabulation is a political process because it constitutes or invents a people who oppose established fictions, or majoritarian oppression. 'A people', he notes, 'is always a creative minority, and remains one even when it acquires a majority: it can be both at once because the two things aren't lived out on the same plane' (1995: 173–174). Instead, '[w]hat defines the majority', he argues, 'is a model you have to conform to: the average European adult male city-dweller, for example... A minority, on the other hand, has no model, it's a becoming, a process' (1995: 173). Indeed, it is worth noting that Deleuze formulates his explanation of fabulation, quoted above, as '*the movement* of constitution of a people' (my emphasis).

For both Bergson and Deleuze, movement is central to how fabulation functions as mediation/through mediators. Mullarkey describes Bergson's work on vitalism in terms of 'how we perceive movement as something life-like, and why we do so' (2007: 54), with fabulation providing a way to grasp how life is mediated through myth-making and 'the paradox of fiction'. He expands his argument through an analysis of film, proposing that '*filmed* fiction is an exemplary instance of this make-believe, because it exploits one of the main conditions necessary for such a "willing suspension of disbelief", namely *movement*' (2007: 54). For example, he argues that through the moving film image, fiction is both real and unreal:

cinematic perception differs from and undermines our normal, everyday perception. I am shocked by the image of the train approaching me, not because I believe it is a train (if I did, I would leave my seat and run), but because of the *material* impact of the image itself (so I hide my eyes). (2007: 65)

The movement of the cinematic image is here affective – registering both perceptually and materially. Moreover – and importantly for my discussion so far regarding *future* politics – Mullarkey analyses the Hollywood blockbuster film *Titanic* and points out that:

our 'willing suspension of disbelief' in fiction lies not simply in the *artifice* of fabricating *fact*, but also in fabricating *time*, bringing to the image (constructed in the past), the 'illusion of the present tense'. But this phrase, the 'illusion of the present tense', which James Auge used to describe Italian neo-realism in particular, may be generalised. Hoping to change the event of the Titanic's collision doesn't come only from making the event live and feel, but also from having it present, reliving its present, and so reopening its future. We believe we are seeing it happen *now*, and it is from *this* temporal state of *actuality* that our paradoxical beliefs, desires, and so on, may follow. One could argue that fiction-making is, by the same token, present-making, for the present, broadly understood, is what is alive for Bergson: movement is actuality and animation (literally), for to move is one condition of being alive that, primitively, allows us to animate things even further. (2007: 66)

Fabulation, here, is 'present-making' in that 'it makes the event live and feel' and makes it present. This is movement that is at the same time 'actuality and animation', 'happen[ing] *now*' and opening the future of the event.

In this example, the past 'real' event of the ship sinking is relived and, paradoxically, although we know the outcome of this 'real' event, we want to stop and change it – to change its future. This future-orientation of fabulation is developed further by Deleuze and Guattari, for whom fabulation refers not necessarily to a past or real event, but is oriented more towards the creation of a discourse or collective. They argue that '[c]reative fabulation has nothing to do with memory … In fact, the artist … goes beyond the perceptual states and the affective transitions of the lived. The artist is a seer, a becomer' (1994: 171). Thus, as Roland Bogue (2010) explains, for Deleuze, '[f]abulation's specific mode of becoming is that of fashioning larger-than-life images that transform and metamorphose conventional representations and conceptions of collectivities, thereby enabling the invention of a people to come' (2010: 100).[5]

Considering the politics of fabulation and offering a slightly different version of the relationships between presents and futures with his concept of Afro-fabulation, Tavia Nyong'o (2019) argues that fabulation involves 'incompossibility', or the 'tether[ing] together of worlds that can and cannot be' (2019: 6). These worlds that both are and are not possible exist at the same time – Afro-fabulation is not so much directed towards the making of a better future as it is concerned with participating in the simultaneous revelation and invention of 'another world [that] is not only possible, [but] is virtually present' (Nyong'o 2019: 18). These framings of fabulation as present-making, future-oriented and imaginative resonate with those of queer theorist José Esteban Muñoz's (2009) conceptualisation of hope. Muñoz's understanding of hope is developed in the context of a concern with the politics of queerness, which he argues are often limited by a focus on the present – on what queerness is. Muñoz opens up the temporalities of queerness, arguing that 'queerness is primarily about futurity and hope' and that '[q]ueerness is not yet here' (2009: 1). In other words, queerness is a future-oriented politics.

---

5 An important point to note is that for Bergson, fabulation is fundamentally a negative process, in that it refers to 'closed societies' that function through religion, for example, which blocks the development of social bonds that create alternative societies (see Bogue 2006). In taking up Bergson's concept and insisting on a politics to it, Deleuze's interest is in how fabulation may be involved in the creation of such alternatives.

For Muñoz, there is an intimate connection between politics, futurity and hope, in that hope is an 'affective structure ... that can be described as anticipatory' (2009: 3) and can open up future possibilities. Muñoz goes on to describe this affectivity of hope as an 'anticipatory illumination ... a kind of potentiality that is open, indeterminate, like the affective contours of hope itself' (2009: 7). Hope here is *potentiality* – 'a certain mode of non-being that is eminent, *a thing that is present but not actually existing in the present tense*' (2009: 9, my emphasis). As with Hawkins' account of the temporality of the single-use PET water bottle, anticipation is here understood in terms of a folding together of the present and future. For Hawkins, the future (waste) of the PET bottle is already anticipated in its design and use; for Muñoz, anticipation is a potentiality or illumination in the present that indicates the possibility of a different, and better, future – a state, condition or quality that both exists in the present but is not quite or actually present. In this sense, hope is open and indeterminate; it indicates a future that cannot necessarily be known but is nevertheless felt in advance of its actualisation or materialisation. Importantly, the potentiality of hope is affective – it is intangible and yet it is *felt* – and it is through this affectivity that a future politics of queerness are produced and organised. Muñoz's argument about hope, then, brings some further clarity to the politics that might be involved in fabulation, for the 'insistence on potentiality or concrete possibility for another world' (2009: 1) is necessary because '[t]he here and now is simply not enough' (2009: 96).

Muñoz's argument is concerned specifically with queer politics; putting his argument into dialogue with the political implications of a fabulation involving anticipating and creating the future in the present indicates that it is productive both in terms of minoritarian politics more generally (Coleman 2017a), and what Davina Cooper (2013) calls 'everyday utopias'. For Cooper, everyday utopias are 'networks and spaces that perform regular daily life, in the global North, in a radically different fashion' (2013: 2). Against an abstracted idea of utopias – as perfect and unobtainable – Cooper understands everyday utopias as prosaic and focused on 'what is doable and viable given the conditions of the present. Yet everyday utopias also capture a sense of hope and potential, in that they anticipate something more, something beyond and other to what they can currently realise' (2013: 4). In these ways, as a means of making futures within the present, these everyday utopias can be understood as a mode of pre-figurative politics, which, as Cooper puts it, involves 'the merging of means and ends' so that 'present-day life [is performed] in terms that are wished for, both to experience better practice and to advance change' (2017: 335).

Indeed, what I want to suggest in this book is that a future politics of glitter can be understood in terms of hope, fabulation and pre-figurative politics; that is, I see the cases and examples I explore as divergent, everyday yet potentially hopeful attempts to provoke different and better worlds. Further, while the focus of Deleuze's and Deleuze and Guattari's accounts of fabulation are on art and artists, I want to consider how non-human entities – in this case glitter – might be involved in fabulating futures, picking up on their suggestion that 'things too' can be mediators. In these ways, I examine the multiple future politics that glitter sets off, exploring how fabulation and hope do not always succeed, or at least do not always succeed in a readily accessible way. At the same time as I explore these hopeful future politics, I also aim to hold on to the dystopian futures that a politics of plastic-as-waste demand are taken seriously. The chapters and interventions therefore attend to the panoply of politics that glitter, and plastics more widely, generate, seeking not to determine a cohesive or complete position on them but to highlight their diversity and open-endedness.

3

Shimmering Futures: Girls, Luminosity and Collaging as Worldmaking

Media praxis, in Juhasz's words is the 'making and theorising of media towards stated projects of world and self-changing', and can be a vital component of feminist and/or queer political action. (Fotopoulou and O'Riordan 2014)

Imagination is our sensory experience of the world, an experience that is a kind of collective awareness, as our bodies are an extension of our contexts. (Hickey-Moody, Harwood and McMahon 2016: 30)

To approach objects like stickers, Hello Kitty, and glitter solely in terms of their significations doesn't tell us much about ... what they do to bodies. (Swindle 2011: 31)

In Chapter 1, I introduced a methodology of following the thing, and discussed how glitter, as a thing, emerged as particularly vibrant and seemed to demand me to follow it. I located this emergent vibrancy in workshops with teenage girls, conducted in July 2016 at a girls' school in southeast London, which involved twelve girls collaging imaginations of their futures. In designing the workshops, I was interested in developing a methodology for imagining and engaging (with) futures. While I had bought tubes of glitter alongside other crafting materials (see Figure 3.1), I had not anticipated glitter becoming the focus of my attention. However, it seemed to demand that I notice it, and pay attention to it (Figure 3.2). It moved from the collages themselves to human bodies and the class-room, as we and it became covered in glitter (Figures 3.3 and 3.4). Most of this was accidental, but it was also sometimes deliberate (Figure 3.5).

In this sense, glitter was the material that the girls got overtaken with, which is how artist-teacher Clare Stanhope from Goldsmiths described what had happened in the workshops. In this chapter, I discuss both the collages that were created in the workshops, and the making of the collages and the kinds of affects that it generated. That is, as well as analysing the collages themselves, I also focus on the methodological process through which the girls worked with various media and materials, including glitter. In so doing, I elaborate on the methodology of following the thing, paying particular attention to the issues of vibrancy and affectivity that it raises, and exploring how it crosses boundaries between media and material in its thingness. I also examine the temporal politics that the methodology raises in the context of asking these girls to both imagine and make their futures, and in the understanding of glitter as future-oriented that I am proposing in this book.

The chapter is organised into three sections. The first considers in more detail the specific method of collaging futures and situates this within wider methodological and practice-research moves in feminist new materialisms. The second section examines the affective relations between glitter and the girls in terms of the centrality of glitter to mainstream-media girl culture, and especially how it functions to indicate luminosity, sparkle and love. In this section, I analyse some of the collages produced in the workshops. The third section returns to the issue of the affective appeal of glitter to the girls who participated in the workshops, and to Bennett's arguments about vibrancy, enchantment and wonder that I discuss in Chapter 1. In suggesting that there is a vibrant engagement between glitter and these girls, I consider further what this might indicate for under-standing the specificity of certain things, and how they may attract and lure certain bodies. In so doing, I also return to the concepts of fabulation introduced in the previous chapter, developing it by way of these empirical examples.

Collaging Futures as Methodology

The 2016 workshops were deliberately conceived and run to develop a methodology for engaging (with) futures. According to the latest Ofsted report on the school, it is based in a disadvantaged area of London. More than twice the national average are known to be eligible for free school meals. Approximately 85 per cent of students are from minority-ethnic

backgrounds, with Black Caribbean and Black African heritages composing the largest groups.[1] Twelve girls in year 9 (aged 13–14 years old) who
came from a range of racial and ethnic groups participated in the collaging
workshops. I worked closely with the arts teacher in the school and we
arranged for the workshops to take place over two consecutive days. They
were held during the usual, timetabled arts lessons in the arts classroom.
The workshops were approved by the head teacher at the school, and by
my institutional research ethics committee. Informed consent forms were
signed by both the girls and their parents/carers. The workshops were
audio-recorded and I also took photographs and recorded some video
during them.

The workshops were structured around a number of exercises.
I gave a handout to the participants (below) and we worked with this
as a basis.

SESSION 1

Exercise 1: Imagining yourself now, in the present

Imagine yourself now, in the present.

How would you describe yourself?

For example, you may want to consider the kind of person you are,
your family and friends, where you live, what you like doing.

You may want to sit quietly for a while, to begin to do this

You should then begin to note down words or sentences to help
with this imagining, and/or you may want to sketch or draw or doodle.

Exercise 2: Imagining yourself in the future

Imagine yourself in the future.

What are your dreams, hopes, aspirations for your future? What
kind of person do you want to be?

---

1 Ofsted is the Office for Standards in Education, Children's Services and Skills. It carries out
regular inspections of schools, and its judgements and reports form the basis of school
league tables.

Again, you should then note down words or sentences to help with this imagining, and/or you may want to sketch or draw or doodle.

Exercise 3: Collaging 1

Begin to go through the different materials here. Select the materials you would like to work with to collage these imaginations. You may make one collage or multiple ones.

How will you try to collage your imaginations of your present and future?

Questions to consider:

What kind of background will you have?

You can select from different-sized paper, canvas, or work with an existing magazine page.

What kinds of materials will you use from what has been provided?

Try to think about your reasons for selecting these different materials.

Will you incorporate your notes or jottings into your collage/s?

If you have time, you can begin working on your collages. You can continue tomorrow, so don't worry if you don't get far on them.

Packing up

Please hand in your informed consent forms – please remember to have signed them, and to have included whether you would like me to use your name or an alias.

SESSION 2

Collaging 2

Work on your collages – imagining your presents and futures.

Discussions

Please remember that this discussion will be recorded. If you have any questions on this, please let me know.

Introduce your collage to the rest of the group.

Say something about your imaginations of your present and future.

Say something about the materials you've used – why did you select these materials?

What did you like about using these materials? What did they enable you to do?

What didn't you like about using these materials? What did they restrict or limit?

Did you use specific techniques (e.g., cutting, tearing, folding, gluing)? Why?

Is there anything else you'd like to say about your collage?

The workshops drew on research with collaging that I had previously conducted on how teenage girls experienced their bodies through images (Coleman 2009). Working with 13–14-year-old girls, I organised two image-making sessions where the girls collaged images of their bodies through materials from different sources, including magazines, a Polaroid camera, craft materials, make-up and sweet wrappers. I understood these collages through the notion of assembling and assemblage (Deleuze and Guattari 1987). The collages made by the girls are constituted by materials taken from various sources, which are arranged in ways that demonstrate how they have been transformed in the move from one source and setting to another (e.g., from a magazine to a collage, from mass media to a classroom to various academic publications), and in the relations the parts have with each other (e.g., through how they may be juxtaposed, and/or organised so as to create a particular impression or sensation).

Furthermore, in these collages, issues concerning change were highlighted. For example, some girls, including Anna, highlighted how understandings of a person may change depending on whether they are based on looks and appearance or 'what's inside'. Others juxtaposed photographs of themselves with images from mainstream women's magazines; for example, Fay wrote 'I wish' next to images of celebrities, indicating what she experiences her body to be, and what she would like it to become. In these cases, then, the issue of change and transformation – the future-orientation of their bodies – is key.

Given these themes regarding change and the future that emerged in these previous workshops, and how collaging involves the assemblage of a range of media and materials, I deployed a collaging method in July 2016 with more 13–14-year-old girls, this time asking them specifically to image their imaginations of their futures. I understand collaging as a material and temporal method, that is, a method that materially engages time. Engaging here refers to how somebody or something becomes involved in and attracted to somebody or something. In this case, collaging is a technique that engages teenage girls.[2] It is a familiar activity from arts classes and popular culture (e.g., magazines, adverts) and may be done at home individually or with friends. It is also a temporal method, or a method that engages futures, in that in 2003 change and transformation emerged as a key constituent element of the assemblage – and this was deliberately mobilised in 2016. Collaging became a way to imagine futures through the process of making. It became a method to potentially bring together different temporalities, imaginations, wishes, desires on one surface.

The collaging methodology can be understood within a wider series of developments in social science methods and in feminist new materialisms. One important aspect of the new materialisms is an understanding of the world as open-ended, and with the potential to become different/ly. Materialities are future-oriented temporalisations, where temporality is non-linear; the future is not that which inevitably unfolds from the past and present in a causal fashion, but is better understood as a virtual possibility that may, and may not, be actualised (e.g., Grosz 2013; Coleman 2009, 2014a, 2014b). Crucial here is that, as Karen Barad notes, 'the future is radically open at every turn' (2007: 178) – that is, agency has the capacity for change and transformation. However, what also needs noting are the ways in which this radical openness may not be actualised, and that it may be difficult for some transformations to take hold. Until recently new materialisms has been a largely theoretical or conceptual field.

2 And not only girls! I have been working with collaging in a range of research and teaching contexts, including at conferences and workshops concerned with feminist new materialisms and teaching on gender, media and methodologies, where it has also been proved popular.

However, some approaches to methodologies and research practice/practice research are beginning to emerge (see, for example, Hickey-Moody and Page 2015; Barrett and Bolt 2012, 2014; Page, Palmer and Coleman 2019). Anna Hickey-Moody and Tara Page argue that '[p]ractices, teaching and art production practices are modes of thought already in the act. Contemporary arts practices call us to think anew, through remaking the world materially and relationally' (2015: 1).

Focusing on methodologies and practices is therefore one way to examine how the collaging workshops might be a method to examine, engage and invent ways for actualising futures. To draw on the quotation from Aristea Fotopoulou and Kate O'Riordan cited above as an epigraph, collaging can in this sense be understood in terms of 'media praxis' – a 'vital component' of feminist and queer politics in its attempt to be both 'world and self-changing'. That is, collaging may be understood as a method of worlding. For Hickey-Moody (2013), such worlding practices through arts are especially important for young people as they 'offer ... new qualitative senses through which people, things, or issues might be known, and through calling into being possible future trajectories associated with the specific qualitative states produced through arts' (2013: 124). Hickey-Moody frames this particular view of arts in terms of fabulation, arguing that '[t]he implications that the idea of fabulation has for thinking about art are that projects can only be seen to have made "art" if they create a set of sensations' (2013: 125). Thus, a 'product does not stand as art because it is created by an artist as "art": it is only art when and *if* it makes a new aesthetic sensibility connected to youth' (2013: 125).

Understood through this new materialist perspective, art generates the capacity of 'calling into being possible future trajectories' through the creation of new sensations and sensibilities. Working with young people to make art, Hickey-Moody argues, has the possibility of producing such sensations and thus making new futures, new worlds. Art, understood in terms of fabulation, can 'generate a missing people' as Deleuze puts it (see Chapter 2), or a new sensibility towards the possibilities of young people. In their study of the politics of widening access to and participation in university education, Valerie Harwood, Hickey-Moody, Samantha McMahon and Sarah O'Shea (2016) explore how this might be practised, arguing that it is essential to understand how young people who live in disadvantaged communities imagine and feel about university in order to 'open out the possibilities of educational futures' (2016: 7). They see imagination as central in remaking the world anew through producing alternative possible futures. For example, in interviews, asking young people to imagine a university produced almost uniformly negative ideas. Harwood *et al.* understand these ideas as images that organise and, in the case of negative images, limit futures. They argue that reorganising images through providing opportunities for young people to make different ones is one way of expanding the educational futures that might be possible.

In the collaging workshops at stake in this chapter, I asked the girls to imagine their futures in relation to their hopes, dreams and aspirations, and the kind of person that they want to be. I also asked them to collage – literally image/make images of – these imaginations. This method both produced mainly positive images – as I discuss below, the images involve wonder and enchantment – and was itself a process that produced positive affects, where positive affect is understood as that which enhances a body's capacities to act (in contrast to negative affects that, as the above example from Harwood *et al.* indicates, limit such capacities) (see also Coleman 2009; Hickey-Moody 2013). In these senses, the workshops involved the making of images that expanded possible futures – that worlded in positive ways. Below I discuss how this occurs in the collages themselves; in terms of the methodological processes of making them, at least three points become significant.

A first point to note is that in both 2003 and 2016, the workshops were absorbing and enjoyable activities – for both the girls and me. It was also noticeable how the task of collaging futures and experiences of bodies soon became collective activities – partly because materials needed to be shared, so there was swapping of glue, scissors and so on, and also because certain materials became popular. Drawing attention to a collective or individual sense of enjoyment may seem insignificant but, returning to Bennett's argument about the cultivation of an openness to the affectivity and vibrancy of things discussed in Chapter 1, there is a sense of foolishness, if not naivety, in this methodology. It is important, I would suggest, for methodologies to seek to foster enjoyment, perhaps especially in the context of what Mike Savage and Roger Burrows (2007) call the 'coming crisis of empirical sociology', where methods initially developed by sociology and wider social sciences, such as interviews, ethnography and focus groups, are increasingly employed in commercial sectors. This situation involves the methodological expertise by which sociology has traditionally defined itself no longer belonging to it alone, and new audiences and markets being enrolled in what are often more agile and fun versions of these methods. The question of how social sciences might re-develop their own methods so that they are themselves fun is therefore crucial. Moreover, there is a politics and ethics to how this question might be addressed, which is especially important to note in terms of Kember's point concerning the potential for new theoretical and methodological developments to be complicit with industry (see Chapter 1). In the context of this book, the question becomes one of developing methods that open up and open out the possibilities of futures.

Mike Michael (2012) argues that interdisciplinary methods are particularly productive in doing this. Working between sociology and speculative design, he says, is a means of considering the 'common byways' between these disciplines, their aims and practices, and 'rendering' these in 'open, multiple, uncertain and playful' ways (2012: 177). Here, the emphasis is on a methodology that is 'less a case of answering a pre-known research question ... than a process of asking inventive, that is, more provocative questions where intervention stimulates latent social realities, and thus facilitates the emergence of different questions' (Wilkie, Michael and Plummer-Fernandez 2014: 4). As inventive or performative, methodology is necessarily uncertain, open-ended and multiple. Methodology is involved in the changing of the social reality it seeks to study; it intervenes or interferes with in it (Haraway 1991; Law and Urry 2004; Lury and Wakeford 2012). As this social reality changes, new questions emerge that themselves might demand new methodologies and stimulate new social realities. Methodologies are thus involved in worldings.

Second, such a methodology signals the importance of futurity. Methodology, as I've noted, is involved in the creation of novelty, and in this sense engages the virtual future. This future is multiple, in that it holds many potentialities that may be actualised differently; it is uncertain, in that it is not clear in advance how virtuality may be actualised; it is open, in that the virtual future is never exhausted or finally depleted. The future remains in excess of its actualisations. This point is important in that it draws attention to both the 'radical openness' of the future, as Barad puts it, and to the difficulty of engaging and sustaining the possible futures that may be generated through various methods. My argument in this book is not that the positive affective futures I explore are sufficient in themselves in instigating and maintaining change, nor that they are the only or best way of doing so. I am not suggesting that this book holds the key to social change. Rather, my argument is more modest: that the collaging workshops provide a means to consider the ways in which methods do and might further be able to world affectively positive futures.

Relatedly, the third point is that in considering the workshops as involved positive worlding practices, methodologies and methods *themselves* come into focus (see Lury *et al.* 2018). That is, the methodological process whereby social realities are intervened in and provoked, and where the future may be actualised, come to be at stake. This is particularly interesting from a feminist new materialist perspective, for it can train attention on the thingness of the method, on what's happening and how. In discussing her art practice research, for example, Danielle Boutet (2013) suggests that, 'the artist think[s] through matter, by way of aesthetic/symbolic operations. This is not a thinking process where one finds *answers* to *questions*, but rather where one *contemplates* and *experiences* situations, themes or feeling complexes (or ways of being)' (2013: 30).

I want to note what might be a problematic positioning of the human – as artist or alchemist – as the primary actant or agency within an art assemblage, an idea that I discussed in Chapter 1, where I suggested that things also act and participate in methodological decision-making. However, while there are differences between Boutet's and Wilkie *et al.*'s positions, both challenge the idea of methodology and practice as finding answers to questions – Wilkie *et al.* by positing methodology as the posing of new, inventive questions, and Boutet by seeing the process of making art as one of contemplation and experience. In both cases, there is an emphasis on the research process, which is understood as dynamic and as necessitating thought, reflection and revision or adaptation. In this way, there are connections with Hickey-Moody and Page's formulation of arts practices as 'modes of thought already in the act'. Erin Manning and Brian Massumi (2014) explicate what 'thought in the act' refers to and involves in their argument that thinking, moving, feeling and doing are always already entangled and co-constitutive. Importantly for the focus in this chapter, they develop a speculative pragmatist approach through which they understand research is created. They write:

This idea of research-creation as embodying techniques of emergence takes it seriously that a creative act or design practice launches concepts in-the-making. These concepts-in-the-making are mobile at the level of techniques they continue to invent. This movement is as speculative (future-event oriented) as it is pragmatic (technique-based practice). (2014: 89)

Here, movement is understood in terms of potential: a future-oriented and future-making process that is speculative, notional, uncertain. In this sense, Manning and Massumi's notion of movement, and its centrality to research, resonates with the emphasis I have placed on movement in the book so far, and especially in its significance to my understanding of things as both media and material. It also connects to the concept of fabulation, which has been taken up through the capacities of imagination. Discussing fabulation in Deleuze's work, Daniel Hjorth (2009) explains fabulation as a 'fiction-telling [or] inventing of stories of futures' that contains 'the power to free us from the limits of the present' (2009: 2). He argues that fabulation concerns imagination, understood 'not as a representational power of reason, but as an inventive power presenting images of a world to come' (2009: 3). Imagination 'anticipates and creates the future' (2009: 2), it articulates or expresses ' "nextness", that provokes the world to become something it is not' (2009: 4).

Glitter is significant in how this future world is imagined/imaged. Indeed, while collaging was designed as a temporal method to study change, transformation and futures, glitter emerged from a range of resources as a thing that has the capacity to make futures. There is a particular relationship between the girls who participated in these workshops and glitter, which engaged the future in a positively affective way. This is to understand glitter not as signifier so much as a vibrant thing. Glitter affects. It moves bodies, as Monica Swindle puts it in one of the epigraphs. In the workshops, glitter affectively moved these girls, becoming part of how they could think/make in the workshops, and how they could imagine their futures. Indeed, while glitter features heavily in mainstream girl culture, it does not remain there. As the back cover of the book *Glitter: A Celebration of Sparkle* (Adams Media 2018) puts it,

Once confined to the craft aisle and the hands of children between the ages of three and nine, glitter has migrated to adults of all ages and incomes – who enthusiastically decorate their hair, faces, and bodies with it, bathe in it, and, of course, craft with it. But glitter is more than something you use or look at, it's a lifestyle – a state of mind for people who want to sparkle and shine inside and out. (Adams Media 2018)

Glitter, then, moves and dissipates across ages (and economic backgrounds), potentially attracting adults as well as children. Similarly, 'girl' or 'girlhood' is argued to be elastic, a state or condition that may encompass 'women' as well as 'girls' (e.g., Driscoll 2002). Rather than signifying a specific age range, then, through its relations with glitter, 'girl' may extend from very young girlhood to older womanhood (see also Chapters 4 and 5). In this case, the collages and the process of making them indicate an engagement with futurity through the 'thingness' of glitter – the girls imagine their futures through a thing that both attracts them now and has the capacity to become, to be part of an assemblage of their future selves. In this sense, glitter is a lifestyle. If we think of methods as 'remaking the world materially and relationally', the workshops might be understood as one small way in which the virtuality of futures are imagined and actualised. In incorporating glitter into their collages, perhaps the girls are making their futures shimmer and sparkle.

Glitter and (Some) Girls: Luminosity and Sparkle

It is perhaps not surprising that glitter had a particular vibrancy for the girls who participated in the collaging workshops and that it was a thing through which they could imagine/image their futures, given its position and purchase in mainstream girls' culture. Mary Celeste Kearney (2015), for example, argues that 'sparkle is so ubiquitous in mainstream girls' culture – and so absent in boys' – it vies with pink as the primary signifier of youthful femininity. Thus, girlhood's visual landscape, presented in far more subdued ways just 10 years ago, is now dominated by sparkly brilliance' (2015: 263). Kearney approaches the ubiquity of sparkle in mainstream girls' culture through an examination of how it features in US media and is manifested on girls' bodies through clothes and make-up. She also explores how girls work with and feel about such media, for example, in how girls might 'take ... the pleasures that they find in sparkly media to fashion their own shimmering texts from them' (2015: 271). Kearney thus complicates a divide between media as texts, on the one hand, and (girls as) audience, on the other, asking us to consider the 'materialisations of girls' affective responses to adult-made media', which may 'not easily align with normative paradigms' (2015: 272).[3] In this way, her argument resonates with the notion of glitter as thing introduced in Chapters 1 and 2, where 'thing' refers to glitter as both, at once, material and media, and to its affectivity or vibrancy. It also draws attention to the need to develop a diverse politics of glitter; in not necessarily aligning with dominant paradigms, glitter cannot only be critiqued for its role in re-creating gendered and sexualised inequalities, but might instead or as well be involved in challenging and/or reworking them.

Kearney situates the ubiquity of sparkle primarily in the rise of celebrity culture (2015: 264), which she argues is entangled with transnational fashion trends including those inspired by Hindi films, hip-hop culture and bling (2015: 263). The prevalence of sparkle in these fashion and cultural trends means that 'female youth of all sorts and in all places are hailed by sparkle's assurance to signify a late modern femininity associated with empowerment, visibility and independent wealth' (2015: 264). In particular, she identifies,

a visual trope has been established in contemporary US girls' media, much of which is distributed internationally and thus has considerable global impact: *Either embodying or surrounded by light, young female characters are stylistically highlighted today in ways that make them visually superior to virtually all else in the frame.* (2015: 264–265, emphasis in original)

---

3 Kearney's discussion of sparkle is concerned with theories of postfeminism, and with how structure and agency are understood within them. While postfeminism is not my focus here, it is important to note, especially in terms of the concept of luminosity that Kearney works with and I expand on below.

She notes a kind of luminosity or shimmering presence that occupies and accompanies girls in mainstream media culture (see also McRobbie 2009) and argues that '[e]arly twenty-first century American girls' media are *literally* luminous in their bedazzling, spectacular displays of girlhood' (2015: 267).

Taking up this idea of luminosity, Kearney develops a 'taxonomy of sparkle' (2015: 268), which she argues operates through three different modes: (i) magic, 'produced through animated special effects' (2015: 268); (ii) environmental, '[p]roduced via twinkling stars, flickering candles, and shimmering lights, this form is used to signify a girl's first romance' (2015: 268) and; (iii) 'the adornment of girls' bodies via glittery makeup, sequined clothing and bejewelled accessories' (2015: 269). In Chapter 4, I discuss the adornment of young women's bodies with glitter, and towards the end of this chapter I turn to the relations between glitter, alchemy, enchantment and wonder, in some way addressing the magic of glitter. In the rest of this section, I take up the second mode that Kearney identifies – environmental – and work with it to analyse how glitter is arranged on some of the collages the girls made. I discuss two main ways in which glitter functions environmentally: first in terms of romance or love, and second in terms of framing.

 *Love hearts*

Kearney's explanation of the environmental mode of sparkle focuses mainly on how sparkle accompanies romance – the first kisses and private spaces of young lovers featured in tween films, for example. However, she also notes the attachments girls may have with, for instance, glamorous city spaces and thus extends an understanding of romance from heterosexual relationships between humans to other things (2015: 268–269). In the collages created by the girls, it is notable how in some of them, glitter is arranged in the shape of hearts, or is placed next to a heart with the effect of emphasising it. For example, on one page of words, initially created on an A3 piece of paper as part of the first exercise where the girls noted down words significant to their imaginations of the presents and futures and returned to in the collaging exercise, one participant drew hearts in red, pink, blue, yellow and orange, which appear at the edges of and in the midst of the words (see Figure 3.6).

Purple-and-red glitter frames three sides of the name Cleo, spelled out in purple, blue and pink sticky foam letters, and gold glitter circles the largest heart in the top right-hand corner. The hearts alongside the words and other symbols, including the laughing emoji, a sunshine and palm tree, produce a positive and affectionate affective sensation. Exclamation marks end words, including:

Lips!

Florida = fav American state!

Glasses!

Blue!

Hearts also constitute the dot above the 'i' (Lips!) and bump up against the ends of words (Love, America!, Bermonsey [sic]). Similar techniques are evident on another word collage, also produced as part of the first imagining presents and futures exercise. On this collage, coloured hearts (blue) that end the words 'family', 'Instagram' and 'calls' are joined by a glitter heart at the left-hand side of the page (see Figure 3.7). The glitter heart is relatively small, although its size is in keeping with that of the words, but it is multi-coloured, requiring different tubes of glitter and a layering of different colours, demonstrating that effort has been put into making it.

Hearts also appear on collages made as part of the second exercise, where the girls were asked to collage their imaginations of the present and future. On one collage, made on an A5 canvas, multi-coloured glitter frames the page, and a green-and-silver heart is placed in the bottom right-hand corner. Glitter has also been shaken into the gaps between cut-out parts of women's bodies (Sarah Jessica Parker's face and torso, what appear to be knees in patterned trousers, feet in black, block-heeled sandals and eight different pairs of lips) (see Figure 3.8).

Another glitter heart features on the most elaborate collage made in the workshops (see Figure 3.9). On this collage, also made on an A5 canvas, the multi-coloured glitter heart is visible through cut-out heart-shaped windows on three pieces of paper (white, purple and pink), which are layered and stuck down on their left-hand side. In the middle of the glitter heart is a purple foam letter, 'R'. The bottom layer of white paper is stuck onto the canvas, semi-covering what appears to be the name 'Rochelle'; '2016' has been cut out of a magazine and stuck to the bottom to the white paper. On the middle layer, two dark blue hearts have been drawn in opposite corners of the purple paper, and the letters 'F', 'e', 's', 't', 'a' have been cut out of a magazine, in the same font as in the previous layer. On the top pink layer, two pink hearts have been drawn on opposite corners of the page, and the words 'ESSENCE' and 'NEW ORLEANS LOUISIANA' have been cut out and stuck on. There is a sprinkle of glitter on the left-hand binding. White, orange, pink, purple and black hearts have been cut out and stuck at the top left-hand corner of the canvas.

Of significance here is that glitter hearts are a thing that can be put to work in collaging imaginations of the present and future. In asking the girls who participated in the workshops to imagine their presents and futures and then to visualise – through collaging – these imaginations, they selected media images (from the magazines) and materials (from those provided) that most affected them – that, in Bennett's terms, were most vibrant. These things, then, are not mute or passive – waiting for the human in order to be animated – but are themselves alive and lively. These vibrant things indicate, as Kearney suggests, that an understanding of girls' love should be expanded from heterosexual relationships with boys, as here a range of things – places, people, body parts, media – are vibrant. The glitter hearts that frame, emphasise and/or accompany these things highlight or make more apparent these affectionate affects. In these ways, the vibrancy of glitter itself, and the arrangement of glitter to emphasise vibrant things, 'make literal the "shimmering presence"' of contemporary girlhood (Kearney 2015: 269) and do so in a way that is oriented around what they see or hope their futures (and presents) involving. Put slightly differently, the vibrancy of both glitter and the things surrounded by glitter are future-oriented; they are productive of affection and love now, and these affects are seen as desirable and capable of enduring into the future (Coleman 2009).

Framing

Above, I noted how the page of one of the collages is framed in glitter; this technique of framing is evident in a number of other collages. However, it is not only the borders of the page that are glittered; in a few of the collages glitter also surrounds images of celebrities, animals, food and body parts that have been cut out of magazines. For example, in one collage, cut-out images of the singers Rihanna and Adele, and the actors Kristen Stewart and Cameron Diaz are bordered in gold, silver, green and purple glitter respectively. A photograph of choco-late sauce being poured onto waffles and ice cream is also bordered in multi-coloured glitter (see Figure 3.10). In another collage, two images of models, an image of a tiger cub and one of a woman's mouth with red lipstick are framed by glitter (see Figure 3.11) and in another collage an image of the singer Nicki Minaj and a white, blonde model featured in a perfume advert are also encircled with glitter. As Kearney notes of the visual trope of framing young female characters in contemporary US girls' media, in these collages it seems that celebrities, food, animals and body parts 'are stylistically highlighted today in ways that make them visually superior to virtually all else in the frame' (2015: 264–265, emphasis in original).

The prevalence of this technique of framing across different collages suggests that it is worth considering further. In an essay on the topic of economic externalities, Michel Callon (1998) discusses Erving Goffman's (1971) concept of the frame as 'establish[ing] a boundary within which interactions – the significance of content of which are self-evident to the protagonists – take more or less independently of their surrounding con-text' (1998: 249). While this notion of the independence of what is inside the frame may seem to imply that it is disconnected from what is outside the frame, Callon notes that 'framing puts the outside world in brackets, as it were, but does not actually abolish all links with it' (1998: 249). Instead,

framing is 'rooted in the outside world, in various physical and organisa-
tional devices' (1998: 249), and, as such, involves a 'network of connections
with the outside world' (1998: 249). Indeed, in this way, framing establishes
a relationship between the inside and outside; 'everything mobilised in
the framed setting guarantees, simply by virtue of its presence, that the
outside world is also present' (1998: 250).

While Callon's explanation of the frame is developed in a discussion of a distinctly different topic, it is helpful for understanding how
the technique of framing celebrities, food, animals and body parts in
the collages functions, and, more especially, functions in terms of luminosity. As Kearney's argument suggests, the glitter framing serves to
highlight these particular images. They stand out and attention is thus
brought to their visual superiority. In this way, as with the technique
of the glitter hearts, they are highlighted as vibrant things; things that
provoke affects and are seen as somehow able to endure into the future.
What the concept of the frame offers is an understanding of the relations
between both the framed images and the 'outside world' and between
the present and future.

In terms of the first point, the glitter frame both separates and connects
the vibrant things and the rest of the collage. In the collage that includes
the image of the chocolate, waffles and ice cream, all of the images apart
from one are framed in glitter. The image without a frame is a small cut-out
of a white, blonde woman in a wedding dress. The images cover words,
written down as part of the first exercise, obscuring what they are and what
they imagine. In this case, the relationships between what is inside and
outside the frame not only highlights vibrant things but also literally covers
up other imaginations of the present and future. Perhaps more significantly, to return to the technique of framing the borders of the collage itself
with glitter, the framing sets up relations between the collage as 'inside'
and the institutional and physical contexts in which they were produced
(workshops, classrooms, school, mainstream girls' culture, London, the
UK...) as 'outside'. One interpretation of such framing would be that,
while the collages are created through these contexts, they must also be
separated off from them; the imaginations that they involve are somehow
distinct from the outside world. The future is imagined in the present but
is different to it.

Enchantment and Wonder

In discussing both the methodology of collaging via which glitter emerged as a vibrant thing, and two techniques – framing and hearts – via which glitter was arranged in and on the collages, positive affects have been central. In the workshops themselves, enjoyment and playfulness seemed to be key. In the collages themselves, the things that appear are accompanied with positive affects and the glitter functions to highlight affection for specific things, and to illuminate the relations of connection and separation between the collages (which include positively affective things) and the outside world (which may and may not be positively affective). So far, I have indicated that positive affects are one way in which the possibilities of the future may be opened up. To expand on this idea, it is helpful to return to and develop the discussion of wonder and its relationship to fabulation (Chapter 2). There, I argued that plastic, since its emergence, has been partly understood in terms of wonder and that wonder is also key to an understanding of the ethics of matter – as Alaimo notes, matter can be defined as a 'subject of concern or wonder' (2010: 2). Understanding wonder in these ways is productive for the study of glitter in that it is also imbued with – at least in the cases discussed here – positive affects and sensations.

Maggie MacLure (2013) writes about wonder in a chapter on the coding of interview data, where she discusses 'moments of disconcertion', such as a participant's silence, that were difficult to categorise and incorporate into a coding schema. She describes how her research team 'learned to welcome and pause at these moments', coming to understand them as 'things that gradually grow, or glow, into greater significance than others, and become the preoccupations around which thought and writing cluster' (2013: 174). These glowing data or 'literally hot-spots, [were] experienced by us as intensities of body as well as mind – a kind of glow that, if we were lucky, would continue to develop' (2013: 173). MacLure moves this discussion of the intensive feeling of glowing data into an understanding of wonder. She says:

Wonder is a liminal experience that confounds boundaries of inside and outside, active and passive, knowing and feeling, and even of animate and inanimate. If I feel wonder, I have chosen something that has 'already' chosen me. Wonder in this sense is indissolubly relational – a matter of strange connection. It is moreover simultaneously Out There in the world and inside the body, as sensation, and therefore is distributed across the boundary between person and world. (2013: 181)

While not exactly the same thing, MacLure's notion of wonder resonates with Jane Bennett's (2001) concept of enchantment, which she wants to restore to the condition and experience of modernity. 'To be enchanted,' Bennett writes, 'is to be struck and shaken by the extraordinary that lives amid the familiar and the everyday' (2001: 4). Glitter might be such a thing: a familiar and everyday agentic material that attracts, enchants, engages. It began to gain significance – to glow – out of a range of other materials, including magazine images, pens, stickers, coloured paper, post-it notes etc., and, as I've suggested, blurred any straightforward lines between presents and futures (e.g., the extended state of girlhood) and between the chooser and the chosen.

Moreover, Bennett explains,

Enchantment is something that we encounter, that hits us, but it is also a comportment that can be fostered through deliberate strategies. One of these strategies might be to give greater expression to the sense of play, another to hone sensory receptivity to the marvellous specificity of things. (2001: 4)

Here, then, glitter 'hits' the girls through its relationality with the workshops. That is, the workshops might be understood as a 'deliberate strategy' through which the capacity for enchantment is orchestrated. Indeed, the workshops operated through 'the sense of play' and 'hone sensory receptivity to the marvellous specificity of things' – in the case I'm making, glitter.

Even further, Bennett links her concept of enchantment to wonder, seeing it as an ethical way of relating to the world: 'if enchantment can foster an ethically laudable generosity of spirit, then the cultivation of an eye for the wonderful becomes something like an academic duty' (2001: 10). This 'eye for the wonderful' is a noticing and following of those extraordinary yet everyday things that strike us – here, my noticing how glitter 'glowed,' and in the rest of this book following the future politics of glitter to other worlds/worldings. It is also a call to consider making specific opportunities through which enchantment and wonder might be engaged and honed. In terms of the politics and ethics of methods in worlding, then, it is not only important to consider what things are enchanting and wonderful, but also *how* things might become affective and sensational in these ways. This demands a commitment to making or curating the conditions through which fabulation becomes possible – to being open to what things might fabulate and to how they might do so.

4

'Sparkle from the Inside Out': Vagazzling, Vagina Glitter Bombs and Moments of Magic

Glitter

Term describing a womans vagina as having an irresistible attractiveness. After having intercourse with a woman that has a 'glitter pussy', they are almost put under a spell by her beauty and become obsessed with her. The text/call her nonstop until they get to see her again.

'That girl I slept with last night had that glitter!'

#irresistible #glitter pussy #glitter #glitterful #obsessed

By Stephknee, 31 July 2008 (Urban Dictionary: Glitter)[1]

The vulva, along with the mouth, anus, ears and nose, problematizes inside and outside and confounds two-dimensional surface and three-dimensional depth ... Some of its surfaces are clearly outside (the labia majora) and some are inside (the vagina, the urethra) but most – the labia minora, the clitoris, the opening of the vagina – are both inside and outside, or somewhere in between. (Jones 2017: 34)

'I thought it would be cool if we could sparkle from the inside out.' (Von-Kreius cited in Davidson 2017)

As the epigraph from Urban Dictionary indicates, glitter and vaginas have a close and affective relation.[2] According to this definition, glitter refers

---

1 www.urbandictionary.com/define.php?term=Glitter&page=4, last accessed 10 October 2018.

2 Interestingly, an entry on Urban Dictionary notes that glitter is a 'British slang word for asshole/anus/rectum. this [sic] rhyming slang is derived from "gary glitter" the British 70's rocker. gary glitter rhymes with shitter which is another slang word for asshole. Glitter has the advantage of being able to be used in front of parents/teachers etc. "he was taken up the glitter"' (www.urbandictionary.com/define.php?term=Glitter, last accessed 10 October 2018). I return to the links between gay culture and glitter in the following chapter; here it is worth noting that as with the vulva and vagina, the asshole/anus/rectum is also a bodily orifice that confuses the boundaries between inside and outside.

to the 'irresistible attractiveness' of certain vaginas, which can captivate and enchant those who come into their proximity. Despite not specifying the gender of the one who 'become[s] obsessed' with glitter, the mention of intercourse suggests a heterosexual relation and implies that it is a man who develops these powerful feelings. Notable is the collapse of the 'woman' and the vagina so that it is unclear whether the man is obsessed with the woman or her 'glitter pussy', or indeed whether it is possible to make that distinction at all.

Taking up this colloquial definition and the association between glitter and the vagina, in this chapter I develop some of the themes discussed in Chapter 3. In particular, I see glitter in terms of mainstream girls' culture, where girlhood refers to an expansive state or condition that includes adults as well as children. Stretching the boundaries of girlhood into the future in this way enables an attention to the ways in which glitter functions in terms of luminosity and sparkle, as discussed in the previous chapter in terms of teenage girls, and to how in early adulthood, this luminosity and sparkle is framed in terms of sex and heterosexuality. Here, I follow glitter to its adornment *on* and *in* bodies, exploring how glitter is involved in producing a particular kind of heterosexual femininity, which I explore in terms of whiteness and class.

I focus on two case studies of contemporary glitter adornment practices that involve the vagina: the first vagazzling,[3] and the second vagina glitter bombs. Vagazzling – a term that combines 'bedazzling' and 'vagina' to describe the practice whereby a shaved pubic mound is decorated with crystals, glitter and other decorations – became popular from 2010 onwards through its mediation via celebrity culture and reality television. Vagina glitter bombs were a somewhat more limited phenomenon following the launch of Glitter Dust in the summer of 2017 in the US, which attracted a good deal of media attention, if not actual usage. I analyse how the two cases are mediated in a self-help book and on television (in the case of vagazzling) and online on a product website, blogs, magazines and news reports (in the case of vagina glitter bombs). I unpack central themes

3 Vagazzling is also spelt vajazzling. Other than when referring to sources where it is spelt with a 'j', in this book I use the term including a 'g' to draw through its connection to the vagina.

regarding how glitter is disturbing, both in terms of disrupting boundaries between inside/outside, nature/culture and private/public, and in the ways it is gendered, sexualised and classed. I argue in particular that glitter as it is involved in vagazzling and vagina glitter-bombing is framed as both enchanting and as harmful, and that these opposing views operate in terms of a classed struggle over where the boundaries between artifice and nature lie. In short, in the examples I analyse, a middle-class medicalised and/or exasperated tone positions vagazzling and vagina glitter-bombing as artificial, irresponsible and at risk of polluting the natural body.

My aim in this analysis is not to determine whether vagazzling and vagina glitter bombs are appropriate or indeed safe practices, but rather to see glitter as both *trans-corporeal* and as a mediator in the fabulation of futures. Trans-corporeality is Alaimo's concept for understanding the relationality between the human and non-human world, which is approached in terms of the movement between and across sites. In the way that I mobilise it in this chapter, trans-corporeality seeks to account for how glitter practices that involve the vagina work across and 'problematise ... inside and outside and confound ... two-dimensional surface and three-dimensional depth' as Meredith Jones argues in the epigraph (2017: 34). In paying attention to how, in these cases, glitter both troubles and exists 'somewhere in between' (Jones 2017: 34) inside and outside, two and three dimensions, I develop further the conceptualisation of glitter as both matter and media that I have introduced so far. Further, in following the movement of glitter, I examine how vagazzling and vagina glitter bombs fabulate futures; that is, drawing on Deleuze's conception of fabulation as a politics through which mediators create futures whereby minority people flourish, I explore how glitter may be involved in making what might be mundane but nonetheless magical futures.

Vagazzling

In 2010, the actor Jennifer Love Hewitt published a book called *The Day I Shot Cupid*. Written to recover from heartbreak, the book consists of short chapters with titles including 'Flossed and tossed', 'Let's snuggle! The hormone that makes us do so' and 'OMG I'm 30!' that aim to 'ease any past pain, laugh about the hours of life lost on bad dates, and show that we [heterosexual women] are all the same' (2010: 2). One chapter, titled 'It was vagazzling', explains how her post-breakup transformation was facilitated by a beauty therapist telling her about a 'new beauty trend':

It would not only change my outer appearance, but how I felt about myself on the inside. She said it would add a little sparkle to my life. I called it 'VAGAZZALING'. She wanted to put Swarovski crystals on my hoo-ha. (Hewitt 2010: 108)

In the rest of her chapter, and in appearances on various US talk shows from 2010 to 2012, Hewitt describes both the process of 'lying sober and naked while a woman puts crystals on my little lady' (2010: 108) and the transformative affects/effects of it. For example, in the book she writes,

what I saw when the mirror and I met was amazing. The once pale, sad girl who couldn't figure out how to move on from her breakup had transformed into a bronzed sex goddess with the prettiest hoo-ha in my neighbourhood. (2010: 109)[4]

Similarly, on the episode of *Lopez* aired on 12 January 2010 where she discusses vagazzling, Hewitt says,

I was feeling awful, I had been through a horrible breakup and I was like, uh, this is just awful, and I need something to make myself feel better, and it was the one thing I'd never tried before after a breakup, and so I gave it a try and I felt great. (www.youtube.com/watch?v=NnUloWnKjg4, last accessed 2 October 2018)

In the same interview, Hewitt explains that her vagazzle 'shines like a disco ball', and encourages women to 'vagazzle their va-jay-jays'.

Hewitt is frequently cited as the person who popularised the term and practice of vagazzling. According to the Wikipedia entry on 'Vajazzle', the term 'became the most searched term on Google' on the day following her appearance on the talk show, and the top definition of 'vajazzle' on Urban Dictionary includes reference to Hewitt:

---

4 Hewitt was bronzed as the therapist who introduced her to the vagazzle was there to give her a spray tan. Interestingly, in terms of the example that follows, *TOWIE* is famous for its characters having spray tans.

TOP DEFINITION

vajazzle
To give the female genitals a sparkly makeover with crystals so as to enhance their appearance.
Jennifer Love Hewitt regularly vajazzles her va-jay-jay with Swarovski crystals.
#vagina #crystals #va-jay-jay #genitals # Jennifer love-hewitt
By handy_andy January 13, 2010[5]

According to this version of events, vagazzling became ubiquitous (in parlance if not necessarily in practice) via a young, white, heterosexual actor, whose career begun on the Disney Channel and continued into teen dramas, romantic comedies and crime dramas. Focusing on the role of glitter in vagazzling, we might argue that glitter has moved from girlhood into young adulthood, stretching the boundaries of 'girl', as I discussed in the previous chapter. Moreover, to draw further on the discussion in that chapter, Hewitt's explanation of vagazzling in terms of heterosexual relationships and heartbreak and transformations of the body and self can be understood through the taxonomy of sparkle developed by Kearney; as 'bejewelled accessories' (Kearney 2015: 269), vagazzling involves both romance and magic. In one television interview, for instance, Hewitt describes vagazzling as 'bedazzling for your hoo-ha', as 'like having a sparkly secret in your pants', and as 'mak[ing] you feel saucy, and ... it's kind of fun to walk around and think, no one has any idea how shiny it is down there!' (*Conan*, www.youtube.com/watch?v=DLgfEilskfc, last accessed 3 October 2018). Vagazzling in these senses can be understood in terms of the kind of luminosity that Kearney identifies when she notes the 'literal ... bedazzling, spectacular displays' (2015: 267) whereby '*young female characters are stylistically highlighted today in ways that make them visually superior to virtually all else in the frame*' (2015: 264–265, emphasis in original). Here, Hewitt makes herself luminous through vagazzling.

Similar descriptions of vagazzling are evident in the UK reality television programme *The Only Way is Essex* (*TOWIE*, ITV), which is credited with bringing the term and practice to the UK in 2012. Described on the ITV website as '[p]art soap opera, part reality show, *TOWIE* follows the lives, loves and scandals of a group of real-life Essex guys and girls'

5 www.urbandictionary.com/define.php?term=vajazzle, last accessed 10 August 2019.

(www.itv.com/hub/the-only-way-is-essex/1a9310, last accessed 3 October 2018), *TOWIE* is a scripted reality series that troubles the boundaries between reality television and drama. Indeed, at the beginning of each programme, a disclaimer explains that, while 'the people are real' some scenes have been given 'a little added sparkle for your entertainment'. It is no coincidence that this 'part soap opera, part reality show' is focused on 'real-life Essex guys and girls'; indeed, the specific ways in which the 'sparkle' is 'added' to real-life situations functions through stereotypes of Essex culture as artificial and excessive, with what Faye Woods (2014) describes as 'Essex girls [being] dim-witted and sexualised and Essex boys [being] loud and flashy' (2014: 199). These cultural ideas about Essex emerged primarily in the 1980s 'to refer to the Thatcherite aspirational working class – East End Londoners who moved out to Essex after benefitting from economic growth ... Thus, the county is culturally coded with both East End legacies of the working class and aspirational "new money" – an often self-made new middle class viewed as lacking in culturally ratified taste codes ...' (Woods 2014: 199).

Woods argues that this culturally specific understanding of Essex occurs not only through representations – for example, in the depictions of 'an aspirational lifestyle based around excess and its women's constructed femininities (big hair, prominent cleavage, fake tans, and nails)' (2014: 202) – but also in *TOWIE's* conventions and tonal address to its young, knowing British audience. *TOWIE* 'play[s] with excess, artificiality and awkwardness' and 'employ[s] a knowing tone and engagement with camp' (2014: 198), for example, in its cast's unpolished performances as well as its disclaimer about its constructedness. Indeed, this disclaimer offers a 'tongue-in-cheek humour that signals the program's tonal address' (2014: 209). It is read in a voice-over by Denise Van Outen, an Essex-born actress and television presenter, who 'draw[s] on her star persona as glamorous yet cheekily down to earth "Essex girl"'. Van Outen's voiceover,

simultaneously sets out the program's knowing tone and signals its disruption of documentary's 'truth claims'. This thus illustrates Kavka's argument that 'rather than erasing the division between mediation and reality, television programming has been foregrounding its modes of mediation and hence teaching viewers to be savvy about its status as cultural and technical construction' (Kavka 2008: 5). (Woods 2014: 209)

Glitter therefore has a role in this 'foregrounding of [the] modes of mediation' in *TOWIE*. The text of the disclaimer glitters and sparkles and, despite numerous updates, the opening credits also feature shimmering, crystals and diamonds. The campness, excess and artificiality of the programme is also often organised via glitter, as the example of vagazzling demonstrates. In one scene, beauty therapist Amy Childs talks Sam Faiers and Harry Derbis through the steps of how to do a vagazzle. Woods describes Childs, who along with Faiers and Derbis was a central character in the early series of the show, as,

highly performative in her manner, drawing on camp's favouring of the strongly exaggerated and illustrating Sontag's argument that to 'perceive camp in objects and persons is to understand Being-as-Playing-a-Role' ... Like all *TOWIE* cast members, Amy wears full makeup and blown-out hair whether at a club, at work, or gossiping in a friend's living room ... Amy plays the role of 'Amy Childs', the celebrity she desires to be but not yet is. At her bubblegum pink home salon, she offers a giggling pose of straight-talking airheadedness, seriously yet clumsily talking through the treatments she gives to her friends as she 'performs' her role as beautician. She wears impractically high heels, her brightly dyed red hair clashing with her pink, tight-fitting uniform, which prominently displays the cleavage of her fake breasts. (2014: 207)[6]

Such a 'performance' is evident in a later scene, which shows Childs applying a vagazzle on Faiers, while they describe it as 'pretty', 'like a rainbow' and speculate on what another main character, Mark Wright, would make of it ('I bet he'd like it though').[7]

In these ways, the content and format of the programme link glitter, romance and magic along the lines of what Kearney identifies. As Childs explains that vagazzling begun in Los Angeles and that a lot of celebrities have it done (including, presumably Hewitt), they also highlight Kearney's point about the centrality of glitter in mainstream girls' culture as emerging through celebrity culture and the future that vagazzling promises; Amy 'plays the role of "Amy Childs", the celebrity she desires to be but not yet is'.

6 I discuss Sontag's essay on Camp in Chapter 6.
7 www.youtube.com/watch?v=qGp4eNiYYdQ, last accessed 3 October 2018.

In stretching the boundaries of girlhood into (young) adulthood, vagazzling emphasises not only romance (the first kiss that Kearney points to), but also (hetero)sexual sex and sexuality. In the Lopez interview with Hewitt, for example, he asks of the practice, 'But that seems kind of irritating for the dude?', to which Hewitt replies to much laughter and applause, 'I've had no complaints'. Similarly, on *Conan*, Hewitt replies to the host's questioning of a man being shocked by the 'silver mine down there', with, 'yes, it gets a reaction!' The reference to Mark Wright, one of the serial cheaters in *TOWIE* who at the time of the filming was in a long-term relationship with another central character and is now married to soap-opera actress Michelle Keegan, also demonstrates this aspect of vagazzling. At the same time as a woman may be vagazzled in anticipation of a sexual encounter, the practice is also described in post-feminist terms as 'for yourself'. On *Conan*, Hewitt notes that '[i]t doesn't always have to be done for a man, it can just be done for yourself, to feel special and cute and whatever'. For Childs, a photo shoot with the national tabloid newspaper the *Mirror* where her naked body is vagazzled is accompanied by an interview that treads a careful line between 'the "Essex slapper" stereotype' (i.e., sexually promiscuous) and being 'family oriented' (e.g., her parents approving of her choice of partner) (*Mirror* 2011). The article notes that 'although she's happy to strip down to her birthday suit [for the shoot] today, she wouldn't have done it without the crystals covering her modesty. "I've never wanted to do topless", she vows'. A quotation from her later in the piece notes, 'If I was doing topless, [my boyfriend] wouldn't agree, but he likes me doing classy things. I must admit, if he didn't like something and I wanted to do it and my management said I could, I'd do it! Luckily, we all agree'.

Vagazzling, then, is both 'done for yourself' and to 'get ... a reaction' from a male lover. It is 'a sparkly secret in your pants' and is potentially something more public to which boyfriends and management must agree. In these ways, vagazzling and its mediation in popular culture complicate the boundaries between inside and outside, private and public. Jones develops her argument regarding the capacity of the vuvla to both trouble and exist 'somewhere in between' the outside and inside through an analysis of labiaplasty, 'a cosmetic surgery operation that constitutes of labia minora reduction and/or labia majora augmentation' (2017: 33).

Jones conceives of this practice, its mediation in popular culture and the reasons that women give for undertaking it as the folding of two and three dimensions, so that two-dimensional images of idealised vulvas are made three-dimensional through the transformation of the flesh, and vice versa. Discussing both interviews with women who have labiaplasty and the self-showing of 'the kind [of vulva] that is currently lauded as perfect' (2017: 39) by Kim Kardashian-West in tweets and advertisements, Jones argues that there is a merging of skin and screen, which she sees as,

a coming-together, of two-dimensional media on one side striving to convey three-dimensional experiences, and of three-dimensional bodies on the other side striving to become perfectly two-dimensional surfaces. Traversing bound-aries between reality and representation and between skin and screen, these 'media-bodies' disturb borders. (2017: 40–41)

In other words, there is a movement between bodies and media, skin and screen, two- and three-dimensionality and inside and outside. Indeed, Jones' reference to 'media-bodies' highlights her longstanding work on 'how contemporary bodies and media are conceptually, visually, and physically intertwined' (2017: 29; see, for example, Jones 2008a, 200b). Importantly, Jones argues that to understand 'complex cultural objects like labiaplasty we [feminist, queer, media and cultural theorists] need to abandon narrowly reductive politics of representation such as "the media made me do it" narratives, where media and media images supposedly create women's poor body-images, thus making dupes or victims of us all' (2017: 44; see also Coleman 2009, 2012). Rather, she adopts a position that is 'rigorously critical of all media' but that 'takes as our starting points ideas such as reflexive embodiment, self-showing, and media-bodies. All of these modes of inquiry can be developed to examine how relations between skins and screens are affective, expressive, and intertwined' (2017: 44).

Jones' conception of the blurring of and shuttling between skin and screen, body and image is helpful in returning to and developing the conception of glitter as both, at once, material and media. Her argument emphasises how skin and screen communicate and express through the materiality of their surfaces. Moreover, this is a materiality that is both internal and external, where bodies become 'screens for the self'

(2017: 40). Understood in the light of these arguments, rather than being 'just' a mode of body adornment, vagazzling communicates both personal wishes and desires (I am pretty, I am (on my way to being) transformed (after a breakup), I am ready for a (heterosexual) encounter) and trends in media culture whereby self-expression and self-transformation are increasingly embodied, mediated and self-shown (through media) (Heyes 2007; Coleman 2012).

This latter point is perhaps especially important to note in the context of how vagazzling is classed as well as gendered. As the analysis of *TOWIE* indicates, vagazzling is understood by the cast as both something fun and pretty, and as 'classy', linked with US celebrity culture and hence as aspirational. While one approach to vagazzling on *TOWIE* would be to see it as a superficial practice done by young women who are exploited by mainstream notions of femininity, heterosexuality and celebrity and consumer culture, taking up the position that Jones describes as beginning with 'reflexive embodiment, self-showing, and media-bodies' enables an appreciation of how for working-class women, the body is often the place whereby hopes and desires may be expressed and through which they may be achieved (if somewhat unstably). Indeed, the confusion of the boundaries between inside and outside, public and private that vagazzling involves indicates that the adornment of the body becomes one way of communicating something about who I am, and – crucially – who I would like to become. As Gemma Collins, another central character on *TOWIE*, says of her labiaplasty, 'I'm mega confident because I now have a designer vagina. I paid £2000 and my vagina is perfect now. It looks like something you would see in a movie' (cited in Jones 2017: 42).[8] Vagazzling

8 Important to note here is that Collins is not now 'mega confident'; indeed, her appearances on both *TOWIE* and other celebrity-related media often involve her discussing her lack of confidence. The argument here, then, is not that practices and procedures that involve changing the body result in a stable sense of the self as perfected; rather, they indicate how self-transformation through the body is future-oriented and never complete(d) (see Coleman 2012). Woods' analysis of *TOWIE* is conducted through comparison with another popular youth-oriented reality programme, *Made in Chelsea*, which follows a group of wealthy young people. In contrast to the cast of *TOWIE* who are always aspirational, Woods argues that *Made in Chelsea* depicts 'Britain's golden youth, shielded from life by parental wealth' (2014: 203) and hence in a much more privileged and secure class position. Thus, while the characters of *TOWIE* are aspirational for themselves, in *Made in Chelsea* it is the audience's aspirations that are cultivated.

in these senses is a practice to world a better future, where confidence, happiness or feeling normal (Berlant 2011) is entwined with celebrity and appearance. Glitter here becomes a mediator through which these better futures are attempted to be fabulated. For Deleuze (1995), fabulation is political because it creates a minority who oppose already established stories and models and are instead 'a becoming' (1995: 173). In their grasping of glitter as mediator, the young women who vagazzle work with their association with artifice and excess in a process of self-transformation.

Glitter from the Inside: Vagina Glitter Bombs

One of the ways in which Jones develops her argument regarding the capacity of the vulva to problematize inside and outside is through drawing on feminist literature on the 'leaky' body (see, for example, Grosz 1994; Longhurst 2001; Shildrick 1994). She notes that 'women's bodies are understood in contrast [to men's] as less formed, more subjective, and "leaky", most significantly via the vulva and vagina because of menstruation' (2017: 30). A further way in which vaginas 'leak' is through vaginal discharge, a 'completely normal' occurrence that means that 'you know that "Mother Nature" is doing her thing and keeping your vagina clean', as the website prettywomaninc.com puts it.[9] This explanation of vaginal discharge is on a Q&A page for those interested in purchasing a new product, launched in July 2017, that is described as 'just an alternative for women who find themselves having to wear uncomfortable panty liners all day, every day, because they are trying to prevent that icky, sticky feeling and those embarrassing stains that can damage and ruin your pretty panties'. Passion Dust Magiculate Capsules – more colloquially known as vagina glitter bombs – are 'the first product of it's [sic] kind EVER'. They are,

a small sparkleized capsule that dissolves when you insert it into your vagina the magiculate formula inside the capsule mixes with your vaginal fluid so that whenever you have natural discharge it will sparkle. The result is what we call 'magicum'.

Passion Dust, then, does not solve the 'problem' of vaginal discharge – rather, it makes discharge sparkle.

9 This website was last accessed on 4 October 2018.

Perhaps unsurprisingly, Passion Dust Magiculate Capsules have pro-voked much attention. According to their manufacturer, Lola-Butterflie Von-Kerius, who makes and sells them from her home in Houston, Texas, within days of their launch her website received over half-a-million visits and the capsules sold out (Hoffman 2017). To date, the prettywomaninc.com website where they were initially sold lists them as indefinitely unavailable. In an interview, Von-Kerius explains that she 'had the thought to make a uniquely personal product' in 2015:

I saw a T-shirt that said, 'I sweat glitter', and ... I thought, I want to sweat glitter, too. What would be a safe way to glitter from the inside? That's when the idea for Passion pills hit. I mixed up a batch [of Passion Dust], placed it inside myself and forgot about it – until the next day, when I used the bathroom. I looked down and saw the sparkling everywhere. (Hoffman 2017)

While vagazzling adorns the outside of the body, the Passion Dust capsules make it possible to 'glitter from the inside', or, as Von-Kerius puts it else-where, 'I thought it would be cool if we could sparkle from the inside out' (Davidson 2017), a process that involves the glitter moving from the out-side to the inside to the outside again. Notable too is that the vaginal glitter bombs are framed in similar ways to vagazzling by their users. Von-Kerius describes how she 'looked down and saw the sparkling everywhere', and says that '[y]ou can see yourself shine and play with it all day'. One cus-tomer, Kim Chedi, reported that 'I am pleased with the results and the sweet taste and so was [my partner] ... Just boosted same-old to some-thing magical' (Hoffman 2017). As with the explanations of glitter explored above and in the previous chapter, when it is attached to (white) women's (hetero)sexuality, then, glitter involves the romantic and magical.

In these ways, for these women, the affective experiences of glitter are of wonder and enchantment. Returning to MacLure's definition of wonder, discussed in Chapter 3, as 'a liminal experience that confounds boundaries of inside and outside, active and passive, knowing and feeling' and, as such is 'simultaneously Out There in the world and inside the body, as sensation, and therefore is distributed across the boundary between person and world' (2013: 181), we can see how the affectivity of glitter – its sensations – moves across boundaries. Of enchantment, Bennett writes that it is the sensation that 'lives amid the familiar and everyday', and 'that can be fostered through deliberate strategies', including play and 'sensory receptivity to the marvellous receptivity of things' (2001: 4). These accounts of wonder and enchantment can be enhanced further through the understanding of fabulation as the ways in which imagination and creativity register and are lived out through bodies, transforming them in the process. As Chedi puts it, the Passion Dust elevated a commonplace experience into something romantic and pleasing, indicating that glitter can be understood as a kind of 'everyday utopia' – in this case, a relatively mundane way in which 'a sense of hope and potential' (Cooper 2013: 4) is put into play in anticipation of 'something magical'. Glitter adds some sparkle into the 'same-old' everyday. It fabulates a near-future encounter into something that comes alive.

However, not all of the responses to Passion Dust are in this affective vein. Rather than seeing it as enchanting, many responses to the vaginal glitter bombs reported in newspapers, on online popular cultural news sites and blogs, on social media and on television saw them instead as highly irritating. On the youth-oriented BBC 3 website under the headline 'Doctors are warning people not to put this glitter capsule up their vaginas', Tomasz Frymorgen writes,

In what may come as a total shock to some of you, doctors are warning people not to put glitter dust up their vaginas. Why are they having to state the obvious? Well, because an online retailer claims to have sold out of capsules apparently designed to be placed in your vagina so that you and your partner can get your bits glittery when having sex. (Frymorgen 2017)

Similarly, Gigi Engle writes for *Marie Claire*,

You know, sometimes you wake up thinking the world is a magical place and then you read a story about how someone created a glitter bomb for vaginas and all that hope and wonder goes right out the window.

You remember that there really is no end to the world telling women that their vaginas need to be altered, douched, cleaned, trimmed, poked, and changed to suit others. Everything from menstrual pad commercials to 'beautifying' women's vaginas through vajazzling has been used to shame us vulva-owning humans.

So, logically, why not go a step further and just shove glitter up there, right? (Engle 2017)

Notable here is the tone of Engle's and Frymorgen's reports: a tone of being tired and exasperated about both having to 'state the obvious' – that 'people should not put glitter dust up their vaginas' – and needing to defend 'vulva-owning humans' from feeling ashamed of their vaginas. Their tone is in contrast to that of the wonder and enchantment about glitter discussed above, as Engle's comments about 'hope and wonder go[ing] right out the window' demonstrate explicitly. This irritation *about* glitter is compounded by the potential irritation *of* glitter that gynaecologists cited in both of their articles warn about. Dr Jen Gunter, 'an OB/GYN and a pain medicine physician' who 'write[s] a lot about sex, science, and social media' and is currently preparing a book provisionally called *The Vagina (and Vulva) Bible*,[10] wrote a widely circulated blog post with the simple title, 'Don't glitter bomb your vagina' (Gunter 2017). In it she notes the lack of an ingredients list and speculates on the risks of using the vagina glitter bombs and the possible medical outcomes:

The glitter could be cosmetic grade glitter (tiny pieces of plastic) suspended in some unknown goo of unknown osmolality. It also could be 'edible glitter', which is sugar ... Could the plastic be a nidus for bacteria? Sure. I've seen nasty inflammatory vaginal discharge from sand so this could be a similar set up. Might the little flakes of plastic produce vaginal wall granulomas? (A granuloma is walled off inflammatory mass produced by tissue in response to a foreign body.) They could.

If it isn't plastic and it's sugar, well, depositing sugar in the vagina lets the bad bacteria go wild. Studies looking at treating bacterial vaginosis with vaginally administered probiotics were halted because the glucose keeping the probiotics alive made the bad bacteria go wild.

Could the vehicle be an irritant and cause a vaginal contact dermatitis? Yes and ouch. Think vaginal sunburn!

Is it possible the goo might damage the good vaginal bacteria leading to infections as well as an increased risk of STIs? You bet. Given how tacky it looks it is unlikely an intimate lubricant (or a safe one anyway).

What impact will this have on vaginal pH? Unknown. (Gunter 2017)

In addition to these possible medical conditions, as with both Engle's and Frymorgen's reports, Gunter also notes the potential body-shaming aspect of the vaginal glitter bombs: 'Vaginal injury and granulomas aside

10 https://drjengunter.wordpress.com/about-me/, last accessed 10 October 2018.

the point of the vaginal glitter appears to be "for him", you know because a vagina au naturel just isn't enough. I hate, hate, hate the messaging behind this (and all other vaginal "enhancement" products). Why do we have to shame women inside and out?' (Gunter 2017).

The affect of irritation is not only tonal – 'you know because a vagina au naturel just isn't enough' – but also applies to the physical properties of the glitter in the capsules, whether it be a plastic or sugar, and the potential harm it could do to the vagina: 'ouch. Think vaginal sunburn!' Notable too is the speculative mode of Gunter's warnings. Not knowing the ingredients list when she published the blog post, the medical outcomes are framed in terms of questions and responses: if it is this, could it cause this? Maybe. Two days after the initial post, Gunter updated it to say that 'Someone has included the ingredient list below [in the comments] and this is supposedly edible glitter, so a sugar. I would want to see studies showing it has no impact on vaginal flora before anyone used this. I would also want to see the osmolality, as products with a high osmolality can irritate the vaginal mucosa'. Even knowing what is in the product doesn't yet guarantee its safety.

Other gynaecologists support Gunter's view of the product. In an article in the *Independent* titled 'Doctors warn against new trend of women putting glitter in their vagina' (Young 2017), Dr Vanessa Mackay is quoted as saying, 'If women place foreign objects inside their vagina, they risk disturbing this balance which may lead to infection, such as bacterial vaginosis or thrush, and inflammation', and Shazia Malik reports,

The starch and gelatin will increase the pH as well as adding sugar to vaginal secretions – which will encourage harmful bacteria and fungi such as Candida to thrive.

This causes increased discharge and a painful inflamed vagina, which causes painful intercourse.

Also the glitter capsules can cause tiny scratches to the vaginal mucosa during sex, again allowing harmful bacteria to infect the vaginal walls. Even worse it's possible that some glitter pieces may even migrate up through the cervix in to the womb lining and have exactly the same effects there. (Young 2017)

The future-orientation of the discourse of risk in these medical warnings thus operates in contrast to that of users of the vagina glitter bombs (and of those who get vagazzled) who are excited and enchanted by their capacity to make sexual encounters more magical. As Malik notes, 'Using a product like this so called passion dust might actually kill off any passion at all' (Young 2017).

Central to these differing expectations of what the vagina glitter bombs might do is what might be termed a struggle over the boundaries between inside and outside. As discussed above, as it is involved in both vagazzling and vagina glitter bombs, glitter troubles these boundaries. In contrast, the gynaecologist's and writers' reports attempt to reassert these distinctions: glitter as a material is one that is ultimately incompatible with the insides of the body – it is potentially damaging. Furthermore, in drawing attention to how the vagina glitter bombs are potentially body-shaming, they also suggest that glitter should not be involved in communicating or expressing something about oneself through the body. These boundaries between the inside and outside function through the dichotomy of nature/culture, where what the vagina is and does 'au naturel' is disturbed, distorted and potentially harmed through the insertion of glitter into it and its secretion from it. Here, then, glitter is understood as culture – artificial, excessive and irreconcilable with nature.

The response by the makers of Passion Dust to these medical warnings about the capsules is interesting in terms of how it conceives of these nature/culture relations. Beginning, '*Well Dur!*', the first paragraph of their 'statement to all media requests for comment' continues:

basically, use at your own risk – as you should with *anything*. We know that 'glitter' is not something commonly used in the vagina but that does not mean that it can't be used in the vagina for the purposes that we have intended Passion Dust to be used for. We do not think that our customers are lacking the intelligence or the ability to discern if they want to use Passion Dust as the adult novelty that it is. No one has to defend what they may want to use or try in the privacy of their bedrooms whether it be toys, whipped cream, candies, powders and everything else that is frowned upon in adult boutiques and issued with warning labels. If you are someone who would not personally use such items or products then that is your choice. Some people like plain vanilla and then there are those who love sparkles!

One point to note from this statement is that, as with the medical reports, Passion Dust is accepted to be cultural rather than natural – 'it is not something commonly used in the vagina' – and is assembled with other cultural products including food and toys. The statement does not refute the location of glitter on the side of the cultural rather than the natural, but defends the acceptability for glitter to be inserted into, or entangled with, the natural; although it is 'not something commonly used in the vagina', this 'does not mean that it can't be used in the vagina for the purposes that we have intended' it to be. This framing of glitter as cultural rather than natural but as suitable and indeed pleasurable to be assembled with the natural is performed in two ways. First, it is performed through its association with other materials and objects that are cultural but that might also be inserted into the vagina. Indeed, in addition to the 'toys, whipped cream, candies, powders' that are mentioned in this first paragraph, the statement goes on to note that,

[w]e would never ask women to use our product against medical advice ... We are in no way saying that you should ignore any possible risk that using Passion Dust could have, our stance on this topic is that there is risk in any and almost everything that you do when you are talking about introducing anything foreign into the vagina. This includes all products; from Passion Dust to everything on the feminine hygiene isle in every major store chain across the world.

The products mentioned in the statement include 'trusted items and products' such as tampons and condoms, which come with 'a 1,000 word leaflet in the box telling you all of the possible risks you could be taking using that specific product as it sits on the store shelves with FDA approval behind it'. Further detail on why Passion Dust does not have FDA approval is included on the Q&A page mentioned above:

NOTHING that contains cosmetic grade glitter can be FDA approved because the FDA has yet to determine if it is even necessary. So even though every major cosmetics company around the globe is using it; in your favourite lip gloss, eye shadow, body powder, and highlighter, it's not FDA approved.

According to the statement, then, it is both impossible to approve a product that includes glitter and it is not helpful to distinguish Passion Dust from other 'foreign objects' that may be inserted into the vagina. Indeed, 'medical professionals are obligated by their oath to advise women against the use of products *such as* Passion Dust or any product that introduces foreign bodies or objects into a woman's vagina'. The second way in which the statement defends the appropriateness of Passion Dust is to emphasise its artificiality. The statement highlights the excessiveness of the capsules, captured in both claiming and asserting the rights of 'those who love sparkles!' to use the product if they wish. Throughout the statement, the views of critics of the product are cast as inexplicable – 'I guess some people just really HATE glitter (*go figure*)' – in contrast to those who 'already know that Passion Dust is a perfectly fine, fun and safe product.'

While glitter is excessive, artificial, fake, the statement refuses to collapse these qualities into those who use the vagina glitter bombs. It is not the women who use them who are in need of education, as the media and medical reports imply, but rather it is 'haters' who need to 'read and research … Please base your decision on what you learn not what you've heard.' Customers' intelligence and capacity to decide for themselves is flagged throughout the text on the website, as noted above. Disclaimers on how the product may not be suitable for all – 'simply because no product is 100% safe for EVERYone so what is safe for some people is subjective' – are also included on the Q&A page, where customers are encouraged to 'exercise your own common sense.' In these ways, the statement performs Jones' argument 'to abandon narrowly reductive politics of representation such as "the media made me do it" narratives', where women are understood as dupes or victims. This is particularly important to note given how the glitter bombs are implicitly gendered and classed, that is, are seen as artificial, superficial and frivolous. The information from Passion Dust about its product is that women know their bodies and, moreover, have the capacity to decide what to do with them. Of particular significance is their capacity to have fun, to play and enjoy pleasure, considerations of which, as Susanna Paasonen (2018) argues, 'despite their urgency in and for people's lives', can become overlooked in approaches to sex and sexuality that focus exclusively on politics and power (2018: 6).

Glitter, Transcorporeality and Fabulation

In this chapter, I have focused on the boundaries between inside/outside, nature/culture and private/public, and how glitter is involved in their reinforcement and/or disruption. An attention to the making and disruption of these boundaries is due to the capacity of glitter to get everywhere, to not remain in one place. Drawing on Alaimo's concept of trans-corporeality is helpful here, for it emphasises the inextricable connections between culture and nature. It makes clear the ways in which nature and culture are always already in relations, and how these relations are unsettled and uncertain, requiring an attention to the politics and ethics they generate. My argument here is twofold. First, it is that, in the cases discussed, the boundaries between nature and culture become a site of struggle that is classed. In this sense, a politics concerned with nature and a politics concerned with culture are entangled. Second, it is that the classed politics of vagazzling and vagina glitter-bombing are at once a future politics.

In terms of the first point, vagazzling and vagina glitter bombs in similar and different ways draw attention to how the vagina is a part of the body that traverses inside and outside, and is debated in terms of when and how it is appropriately private or public, natural or cultural. Working through a definition of the 'va-jay-jay' as natural and pure and thus as needing protection from bodily adornment and foreign objects, the arguments or comments of critics or sceptics of vagazzling and vagina glitter bombs police the boundaries of these dichotomies through an implicitly middle-class medicalised tone. The artificial material of Passion Dust, for example, should not be inserted into the vagina, while vagazzling is either seen as potentially dangerous as well, or as an amusing but ultimately frivolous decorative practice.

In contrast, those who have vagazzles or use vagina glitter bombs offer understandings of both these practices and where they are to be located that are more mobile, flexible and complicated. The vagazzle is both 'for yourself' and for the man of an anticipated sexual encounter; it is both public in its discussion and application on television, and private or framed in terms of 'family values'. It is applied on the outside of the body but communicates something of the person's innermost wishes and desires. Similarly, while Passion Dust is initially described in terms of adding sparkle to vaginal discharge, and hence is framed as personal, later on the same webpage advice is given on how long to insert it prior to intercourse (one hour), and what effects it may have on male sexual partners (both physically and emotionally). In these ways, glitter moves across boundaries, demonstrating that they are not fixed and are not understood and experienced in the same way by everyone. As such, glitter as it is involved in these practices creates a kind of natureculture, whereby the purity of supposedly separate domains cannot be maintained, the fiction of clear-cut boundaries is shown and middle-class assumptions about the purity of nature and the danger of artifice are challenged. The Q&A page of the Passion Dust website is particularly indicative on this point:

There are more harmful glitters, chemicals and additives in your cosmetics, bubble bath and bath bombs and body sprays than what is in Passion Dust. Scientifically, you have already inhaled or ingested more hazardous 'glitter' and chemicals than what is in our capsules. These chemicals have not caused you any significant harm medically because the amount that you have ingested is so small that it would take an extremely significant amount to cause you any bodily harm.

Second, the kind of natureculture that those who engage with vagazzling and vagina glitter bombs create is future-oriented. That is, the politics whereby women who vagazzle and vagina glitter-bomb refuse and rework middle-class fears about and disdain at these practices function in terms of a future politics. Understanding vagazzling and vagina glitter bombs as practices involving glitter as thing suggests that the politics and ethics they raise involve glitter as both, at once, media and material. The materiality of glitter is focused on by those who see vagina glitter bombs as unsafe; glitter is a substance that should not be inserted into the body as its effects are either unknown or will be harmful. With a different inflection, vagazzling is also seen as harmful in that, following Jones, it involves working-class young women becoming victims of media representations, which they cannot adequately decode. Here, future politics concern the potential danger of what glitter can do.

However, for those who engage with it through vagazzling and vagina glitter-bombing, glitter is a material that makes the everyday sparkle, and that is communicative in its expression of their hopes and desires of the women, whether those are to feel confident, to get over a heartbreak, or to gain more enjoyment from an imminent sexual encounter. To return to Kember and Zylinska's definition of communication, discussed in Chapter 1, media are communicative in being orientated to that which they are not. In seeking to materialise hopes and desires, vagazzling and vagina glitter bombs are communicative in the creation of perhaps small but nevertheless significant futures that are different to, better than, the present. Here, then, glitter functions as a mediator of fabulation, a thing that creates new fictions providing the conditions for the emergence of a people who oppose majoritarian (in this case, middle-class) modes of organisation. This is a grand claim to make; however, in taking glitter seriously and following where it goes, attention is drawn to the ways in which worlds that sparkle are already being made.

5

The G-Word: Film, Fantasy and Afro-Fabulative Futures

In November 2018, under the hashtag #JusticeForGlitter,[1] Mariah Carey's fans, known as Lambs, streamed Carey's 2001 album *Glitter* enough times for it to reach number 1 in the iTunes chart. Deemed a flop on its release on 11 September 2001 and during a period when Carey had mental health issues that were widely publicised, the Lambs' hashtag campaign gave the album a new lease of life, with Carey reporting that she felt able to revisit songs from the album after only being able to refer to it as 'the G word' (Sciarretto 2013). The campaign also revived interest in the accompanying film, also titled *Glitter*, which Carey starred in and which was released ten days after the album, featuring songs from it as part of its soundtrack. Loosely based on Carey's own 'rag-to-riches' life story, the film *Glitter* follows lead character Billie Frank (played by Carey) as she develops a successful singing career but also experiences a range of painful encounters and set-backs that cut through a simple trajectory to 'the good life'. As with the soundtrack album, the film *Glitter* flopped and was roundly panned by critics, with one describing it as 'too bland to be good and not bad enough to be a *Showgirls*-style camp romp' (Juzwiak 2016). In this chapter, I discuss the film *Glitter*, focusing not on its quality or position in Carey's oeuvre, but rather on how glitter in the film is closely associated with temporality – most obviously in terms of indicating a better future, but also, I suggest, in

---

1 A number of Twitter users responded to this hashtag by pointing out that for those in the UK, it seemed to refer to justice for the English glam-rock singer Gary Glitter, who was jailed in 1999 for downloading child pornography and in 2006 and 2015 for child sexual abuse and attempted rape.

terms of a more downbeat assessment of the folding-together of the past, present and future.

To develop this focus on the relationship between glitter and temporality, alongside *Glitter* I analyse another film: *Precious Based on the Novel Push by Sapphire*, released in 2009 and directed by Lee Daniels. *Precious*, and the novel *Push* by Sapphire (1996), tells the story of Claireece 'Precious' Jones, or Precious (played by Gabourey Sidibe), an African-American 16-year-old growing up in Harlem who, after being excluded from school for being pregnant for the second time after being repeatedly raped by her father, joins an alternative school. In *Precious*, fantasy scenes highlight the ways in which Precious detaches herself from the violence of her everyday life and imagines a better future. While not functioning explicitly through glitter in the same way as *Glitter*, the fantasy scenes in *Precious* are highlighted through what Kearney, drawing on McRobbie, describes as 'luminosity' – 'clouds of light [that] give young women a shimmering presence' (McRobbie in Kearney 2015: 267 – see Chapter 3). Indeed, Kearney analyses *Precious* in terms of the 'brilliant luminosity' (2015: 266) of the fantasy scenes, as I discuss in more detail below.

As in the film *Glitter*, the luminosity of the fantasy scenes in *Precious* do not function in a straightforward fashion but rather highlight the intricate relations between race, gender, class and the possibilities of imagining and achieving a better future. Indeed, *Precious* has received much academic attention focusing on its representations of race, gender, class and weight (Stoneman 2012), its positioning with a supposedly post-racial American landscape after the election of Barack Obama (Baum 2010) and its narrative, which works with both hope and despair (Kokkola 2013). Other work has highlighted its success with white film and cultural critics and audiences and the problematic representations of Black life in the United States (Frank 2012). I explore some of the different ways in which *Precious* is analysed in terms of race and fantasy, which include differing positions on how far the film shores up and/or draws attention to white supremacy (Griffin 2014; Kearney 2015). I also consider the significance of race and 'mixedness', gender and class in *Glitter*, arguing that these can also be understood as implicated in how Billie Frank is able to experience her future. In this chapter, then, my aim is to extend and complicate the analysis of gender and sexuality developed so far in the book to consider how race and racism is involved in the future politics of glitter. This is especially important in terms of how luminosity involves media conventions that emphasise light and brightness that are associated with whiteness (Dyer 1997). I do this through an engagement with glitter *as a thing*; that is, I continue to develop an understanding of glitter as affective and as both media and material. In this chapter, this involves moving between an analysis of filmic conventions, representations and emotions, feelings and affects.

Glitter: Futures and Pasts

The film *Glitter* follows the mixed-race protagonist Billie Frank, from her childhood home with mother Lilian Frank (played by Valerie Pettiford) – a gifted singer who is also an alcoholic – into a foster home and then to her singing career, initially as a backing singer and eventually as a global superstar; one of the final scenes of the film shows Billie playing a sold-out concert at Madison Square Gardens, New York City. In many ways, then, a prevalent theme of the film is its charting of Billie's achievement of a better future. Invited onto the stage by Lilian to perform a duet, the audience is told that the child Billie is 'going to be a really big star one day', and she works with this talent to create a better life for herself. This 'better' life involves Billie doing what she loves – writing and performing her own songs – and being recognised for this. No longer the backing singer whose voice has been appropriated by the lead singer, nor any longer suffering abuse from her producer partner Dice (played by Max Beasley), she is also financially stable; having lifted herself out of the poverty she experienced with her mother and at the foster home and removed herself from the violent relationship with Dice, Billie Frank is in control of her career. In these senses, *Glitter* tells the story of the empowerment of a female singer. Its politics can thus be understood in terms of a post-feminist luminosity where the appeal of (becoming) celebrity is key. At the same time, however, the film deals with temporality in a more multifarious way, as Billie is shown as a loyal friend who maintains relationships despite the radical changes in her circumstances and as seeking to understand and make peace with her past. Along with the making of a better future, then, the past and its implications on the present and the possibilities of the future are also evident. Here, I want to consider what glitter does to both depict and regulate these temporalities, focusing on glitter as affective thing.

The title of the film clearly indicates the significance of sparkle and shimmer to Billie's story. In the film itself, glitter as thing features in a number of different ways – on clothes and costumes, as make-up and in nightclubs – and is referred to through glittering lights, reflective surfaces and disco balls, among other things. Glitter also functions as a filmic device where the screen fills with glitter between scenes that involve an exciting change to Billie's life. For example, a scene where Billie hears her song ('Loverboy', the lead single from the accompanying soundtrack) being played on the radio for the first time after having signed a record deal with a major label features glitter prominently. The scene opens with a shot that moves down from above strings of lights suspended between the upper levels of shops onto a rainy urban street, and then into the back seat of a cab, where Billie and Dice are shown against a windscreen glistening with rain drops. As Billie and Dice move from the car out onto the street and towards a pay-phone, the rain glistens on other surfaces, including the car. Calling her friends Roxanne (Tia Texada) and Louise (Da Brat) – friends originally made in the foster home and still a central part of Billie's life – the scene shows them in an amber-hued room with lights reflecting from everyday objects, including the window frame and shelving unit. The scene moves back to Billie and Dice celebrating on the street, and cuts to a fullscreen of silver glitter floating down. The action slowly moves down to show Billie in full sparkling make-up, with large shiny earrings and a shimmering piece of fabric pulled over a silver glittery bikini shooting the video to accompany the song. Roxanne and Louise are her backing singers, in short sparkling silver dresses and with matching accessories.

A similar shot occurs later in the film, which moves down from the lights outside an awards ceremony at the Center for Performing Arts where, alongside Lionel Richie, Billie has been appearing, to show her and Dice leaving to attend an afterparty. Billie is wearing a pale pink glittery dress and a fur stole in a matching colour, and appears in the flashing lights of photographs being taken of her. The scene cuts between the awards ceremony on the television and Roxanne and Louise in their apartment getting ready for the party. Roxanne asks Louise what she thinks of her gold sequined cardigan, to which Louise replies that she 'looks like a disco ball … it's too much'.

The function of glitter in these examples may seem to suggest that the film moves unproblematically towards a better future; however, this is not the case. Louise's assessment of Roxanne's 'disco-ball' outfit is that it is excessive. Dice cuts short the time at the afterparty following the awards ceremony, ordering Billie to 'get the girls' and get into the car. There, drunk and envious, he sneers at the compliments and the offer to work together that Billie receives from another artist who performed at the ceremony (and who she later goes on to work with) and criticises her dress, which he bought her, as 'everything is hanging out'. The argument escalates as Dice insults Roxanne and Louise, and ends with Billie reluctantly staying in the car with Dice as her friends leave. Back at the apartment, Dice apologises and seems to recognise his intensifying bad feelings as Billie tells him, 'I don't care about this without you'. Leaving Dice's apartment later that night, Billie sees a homeless woman singing, who she initially hopes is, or mistakes for, her mother. The song, 'Twister' from the *Glitter* sound-track, begins by referencing the tragedy of Billie's life so far and praying for resolution: to be reunited with her mother.

The recognition of her talent, then, is shot through with Billie's experience that those she cares about are more important, or equally as important, to her as success. Towards the end of the film, Dice is murdered by another music producer. Billie had worked with the murderer at the beginning of her career, and Dice is killed for failing to pay the transfer price for Billie that they had agreed (without Billie's knowledge). The murder takes place after Billie finishes her abusive relationship with Dice, but also after she has left him a note in his flat that indicates that she has come to terms with, and forgives him for, his abuse of her, leaving open a possible future for them to reconcile. Billie learns of the murder just before her Madison Square Garden concert, and she walks onto the stage in another pale pink glittery dress, looks around, and puts up her hand to stop the backing music and dancing. As the stage lights dim, smiling sadly and fighting back tears, she speaks to her crowd: 'Everybody out there, don't ever take anyone for granted. Cos you never know when you might lose them. And you may never get the chance to tell them how you really feel'. She begins to sing 'Never Too Far', noting the significance of her memories of her and Dice and the comfort they bring. Later in this song, the lyrics include references to glittering and incandescence, which make some of these memories especially vivid, again bringing her comfort. As these examples indicate, glitter features in *Glitter* to develop an account of temporality as convoluted and contradictory. Glitter is for Billie simultaneously painful and hopeful.

Precious: Fantasy, Presents and Futures

The film *Precious* opens with a shot of a red, possibly silk, scarf swaying from a lamppost under a train bridge, the colour emphasising the greys of the urban environment. As the scarf falls and pigeons fly, the following text appears on the screen with the words in capitals appearing in red:

EVRYFIN IS A GIF OF TH UNVRSS
(Everything is a gift of the universe.)
                    – KEN KEYES JR.[2]

A slim, Black woman wearing a red glittery ballgown with flowers and ribbons in her hair emerges from a bright white doorway with the scarf in her hands. She approaches Precious, dressed in a black jacket with large white dots on it and with red lips and red earrings, and carefully places the scarf over Precious' right shoulder. Both women are smiling softly. Throughout the scene, the woman in the red dress is blurry and tinkling piano music plays in the background. It is clear that this scene is somehow unreal – an impression reinforced with the abrupt shift to the next scene, set in Harlem in 1987, with a ringing school bell and Precious, wearing a black leather jacket and an inexpensive red scarf, walking down a school corridor. Precious' voice tells us, 'My name is Claireece Precious Jones. I wish I had a light-skinned boyfriend, with real nice hair, and I want to be on the cover of a magazine. But first I want to be in one of those BET videos. Mama said I can't dance, plus she said who'd want to see my big ass

---

2 The text here echoes the formatting of Precious' journal writing in the novel *Push*, where Precious writes colloquially and her teacher, Blu Rain, 'translates' her words into formal written English.

dancing anyhow'. As the scene moves into a classroom and we see Precious sitting slumped at a desk at the back of the room, the voiceover continues, 'I like math. I don't say nothing. I don't open my book even. I just sit there. Every day I tell myself, something gonna happen, like, I'm gonna break through. Or somebody gonna break through to me. I'm gonna be normal. And pay attention and sit at the front of the class. Someday'.

The first scenes of *Precious* establish a number of key themes and filmic conventions that appear across the film, including the role of formal education and her mother in Precious' better – or normal – future, someday. These scenes highlight the disjuncture between Precious' everyday existence – her school, the urban environment she lives in, her mother's derogatory comments about her – and her hopes, dreams and desires – 'I wish', 'I'm gonna break through', 'I'm gonna be normal' – and more generally the fantasy scene with the red scarf where someone, her fairy godmother, reaches her. The 'someday' that Precious notes introduces a temporal dimension to these hopes and fantasies, indicating in particular a future that will be better. At the same time, this 'someday' underscores just how unbearable Precious' present is. For example, despite liking math, she is disengaged from it, telling us later in the scene that she spends her time daydreaming about being married to her white male teacher and living in a 'normal' place. She feels helpless to 'break through' despite reminding herself every day of its possibility.

The fantasy scenes that are present throughout the film occur at moments when Precious is experiencing abuse and trauma. The second fantasy scene we see occurs about six minutes into the film, when Precious has returned home to the apartment that she lives in with her mother, Mary (played by Mo'Nique, who won a Best Supporting Actress Oscar for her performance), and is washing dishes. As Mary, just visible sitting in the background of the shot, throws an object at Precious, hitting her on the back of her head, Precious falls. We see her collapse onto a bed and close-up shots of a bare-chested man unbuckling his belt, bed springs squeaking, an egg frying and a cat meowing follow. The scene, taking place in Precious' bedroom while her mother hovers in the doorway, shows Precious being raped by her father, the man saying, 'Daddy loves you'. As the rape progresses, Precious' view of her bedroom ceiling is shown. The ceiling peels back through the boards of the floor above and into a brightly lit shot where Precious, dressed in a red velvet evening dress edged with leopard print and accompanied by her light-skinned boyfriend in black tie, exits a film premier to many photographers and interviewers. Whereas Billie Frank appears overwhelmed by the attention she receives exiting the awards ceremony in *Glitter*, Precious happily signs autographs and tells an interviewer 'I feel great!' as she is lit by the flashes of multiple cameras going off. This fantasy scene is interrupted by a thunderstorm, where rain falls and glistens on Precious' face, and we are returned to Precious lying on the floor in her apartment being woken from her fall by her mother throwing a bucket of water over her face.

Another fantasy scene begins after Precious is pushed to the ground on the street by three leering men, landing on a pile of autumnal leaves. This scene transitions to Precious' fantasy through the leaves – now glistening – falling onto Precious as she dances on a plinth for and then with her boyfriend in an otherwise empty but brightly lit club. The fantasy ends when we are brought back to Precious having her faced licked by a dog. Another fantasy scene occurs when Precious and her newborn son, Abdul, walk the streets. Precious flees the apartment they had just returned to following Abdul's birth, after they were both violently abused by Mary; Mary drops Abdul to the floor and throws a glass at Precious' head, accusing her of taking her lover – Mary's partner and Precious' father – to which Precious responds, 'I ain't stupid! I ain't take your man! Y'all raped me!' Leaving the apartment after this brutal fight, Precious and Abdul walk in the snow and pass a church, and Precious imagines singing with the small congregation. In the fantasy, Precious holds a sleeping Abdul while her boyfriend carries a pet dog. They are dressed in blue robes with yellow scarves around their necks, and they glimmer in the lights from a Christmas tree, exemplifying, Rachel Alicia Griffin argues, 'the U.S. American Dream as a smiling, singing, and swaying side-to-side heterosexual couple replete with baby Abdul and a dog – the same dog that previously marked Precious' humiliation on the gloomy sidewalk now helps to complete her happiness in the glowing church' (Griffin 2014: 188).[3]

---

3 See Edwards (2012) for a more detailed analysis of this scene, and more broadly on the relationship between Christianity and salvation in *Precious* and in longer narratives of Black women's empowerment in 'pop black feminism'.

The fantasy scenes are both transitioned into and themselves feature sparkle, shine and shimmer. These occur not through glitter itself but
through materials that have reflective or illuminating qualities, such as water,
autumnal leaves, snow, fabrics and lights. In this sense, as with the film *Glitter*,
the properties of glitter extend beyond glitter itself and into other materials
and visual tropes – what Kearney, as I discuss in Chapter 3, describes as
luminosity – a set of visual conventions in contemporary girls' culture where,
'*[e]ither embodying or surrounded by light, young female characters are stylistically highlighted today in ways that make them visually superior to virtually
all else in the frame*' (2015: 264–265, emphasis in original). I expand on the
significance of luminosity in relation to a politics of race, gender and class
in the section below. Here, I want to focus on the temporalities of the fantasy scenes, and how these function in terms of luminosity. In some ways,
the fantasy scenes remove Precious from the abuse that she receives in the
present – they provide a respite (mentally if not physically) from the cruelty
and violence she experiences. They do this through depicting Precious' ideal
life. The temporality of the fantasies, then, might be in the future or might
be an alternative present; they exist as a time and space different to her life
now. The luminosity of the fantasy scenes works to separate the ideal and
different from the real and now. As opposed to the often dimly lit reality of
Precious' life, the fantasies shine. However, importantly, luminosity also has
a crucial role in the transitions between real life and the fantasies, indicating
that the fantasies are only temporary and unsustainable moments of relief for
Precious. They do not signal a smooth progression to a better future. Indeed,
in her Black feminist analysis of rape, trauma, incest and affect in *Precious*,
Régine Michelle Jean-Charles (2012) writes of the fantasy scene that occurs
when Precious has been hit by her mother:

The transition from small drops of water to drenched splashing from the bucket
stands as [a] point of analysis. In rape narratives water is often associated with
cleansing and renewal, the survivor's attempt to rid him- or herself of rape, but
for Precious in this story, rather than holding healing properties, water becomes
what brings her back to the dismal reality of her life where she is abused, unloved,
and unvalued. There is no cleansing shower available to heal Precious. (2012: 148)

The fantasy scene set in the church is notable for being interrupted by
shots of Mary, alone in the apartment, ripping down posters in Precious'

bedroom and destroying the belongings on her dressing table. The fantasy ends with a shot that takes us through a window in the church in the shape of a cross, up and out into shimmering snow falling in the dark, which fades into the sparkling lights of the subway train that Precious and Abdul ride while she contemplates a safe place for them to go. Here, religion offers Precious no salvation from her present (c.f. Edwards 2012).

Luminosity and Race in *Precious* and *Glitter*

As Precious, carrying Abdul, walks along the subway platform on the way to a safe place after leaving her mother's apartment, she recites the alphabet. The next shot establishes that Precious has broken into the alternative school, Each One Teach One, that she has attended since being expelled from her public school at the beginning of the film for being pregnant. Through the alternative school, Precious begins to establish confidence. She makes friends with the other young women in her class and learns to read and write, composing poetry so that she can articulate the insights about her life that she already had, and begins to place her life within a broader context of abuse and neglect, as demonstrated by her furious response to her mother when she returns to the apartment from hospital with Abdul and expresses her history of sexual violence and incest – 'I ain't stupid! ... Y'all raped me!' As the film finally removes any hope that Mary will 'break through' and care for Precious and Abdul, another central woman in the film takes on extra significance: Precious' teacher at Each One Teach One, Ms. Blu Rain (played by Paula Patton).

A connection can be made between Blu Rain and the fairy godmother shown in the opening fantasy. Both are figured in terms of colour – blue and red respectively – and both manage to reach Precious, the fairy godmother through the gift of the red scarf, and Ms. Rain through the role of teacher, mentor and carer. Upon finding that Precious and Abdul have broken into the alternative school, Ms. Rain and other members of staff spend the day on the phones, finding them an alternative place to live. Precious and Abdul are eventually offered a place in a half-way house in Harlem – an important location as it means that Precious can continue attending Each One Teach One – but need a place to stay for the night before they can move in. Precious and Abdul spend the night with Ms. Rain and her partner Katherine (played by Kimberly Russell). The evening is depicted as warm and joyous as the three women play Scrabble, drink wine, eat their fill and pass Abdul around, and Precious' homophobic prejudices are dissipated.

One way of understanding *Precious* is to see it as offering education as the route to a better future. Indeed, Precious wins a Mayor's Award for Literacy, and a cheque for $75, and a party is thrown in her honour at Each One Teach One. The scene is shot and lit as if it is a fantasy scene; the transition into the scene is through what looks like a string of lights, loud music is playing and Precious and her friends dance and are photographed, illuminating the room with the camera flash. Discussing the novel *Push* by Sapphire, Lydia Kokkola (2013) notes that '[t]he fact that [Precious] and some of the other girls in the alternative school do manage to improve their lot in life appears to suggest that society can change and that education provides the key to such change' (2013: 394). However, Kokkola cautions against such an understanding of the novel – and hence the film that is based on it – arguing that it 'does not shy away from depicting the long term consequences of Precious' abused childhood' (2013: 394):

Despite the great gains Precious makes in terms of literacy development, her absolute levels of literacy remain so low that she is unlikely to find employment that pays above the minimum wage. More importantly, she has contracted HIV from her father and, given the date when the novel is set, we can assume that she will develop AIDS and leave her son to the mercy of a social welfare system that Sapphire portrays as being deeply flawed. (2013: 394)[4]

The novel and film do not unfurl towards a better future, then, but rather operate according to interconnecting and incompatible narratives of hope and despair (Kokkola 2013: 394–395).

---

4 Indeed, Sapphire's follow-up novel, *The Kid* (2012), depicts Abdul as an orphan at the age of 9 and tells the story of the sexual violence he then experiences.

A prevalent way in which the tensions between competing affects and possible futures at work in *Precious* have been analysed is in terms of racial politics, and especially with respect to how whiteness functions as a privileged position. Griffin (2014) argues that a white-supremacist capitalist patriarchal gaze structures *Precious*. Discussing the fantasy scenes in particular, she suggests that,

we are introduced to [Precious'] idealised life, largely characterised by appeals to light/Whiteness and middle- to upper-class status. Interpreting these scenes via Black Feminist Theory reveals far more than an abused teenager wishing for a better life that she indeed deserves. Hence, Precious' fantasies reveal her imagined escapism as a reconstitution of 'white supremacist capitalist patriarchy' ... – a term offered by bell hooks to name 'interlocking systems of domination' ... Thus, despite the film's standing as a Black cultural production, I argue that Precious' fantasies idolise light/White beauty and the light/Whitening of the American Dream, and subsequently reconstitute racism, sexism, and classism in accordance with the dominant gaze. (2014: 185)

In her analysis, Griffin notes how one way in which this light/whitening works is through how, 'everyone who comes to Precious' aid can be read as light/White' (2014: 187). These characters include the light-skinned boyfriend who appears in Precious' fantasies, the white school counsellor Mrs. Lichtenstein who follows up on the expulsion of Precious from school by visiting her home and telling Precious, over the apartment intercom, about Each One Teach One, Precious' caseworker Ms. Weiss (played by Mariah Carey) and Nurse John (played by Lenny Kravitz), who cares for Precious and Abdul after the baby's birth. For Griffin, 'the primary character in the replication of light/Whiteness as saviour and safety is Ms. Rain' – a 'tall and slender, light-skinned Black woman with straight hair and European features' who is 'one of the few to treat Precious with compassion', and 'sparks a turning point in Precious' life by encouraging her to recognise the power of her own voice through journaling' (2014: 188). Griffin's argument is that,

these characters [are] in alignment with what dominant ideologies mark as good, right, and respectable. Therefore, although visibly present in the considerable 'absence' of Whiteness, each character of colour affirms dominant understandings of Whiteness as superior and Blackness as inferior. The implicit assumption reads: the closer Black people get to Whiteness (i.e. the less 'Black' they are), the better. ... palatable Black characters are typically allegiant to dominant constructions of privilege and marginalisation. (2014: 188)

Other arguments make similar points about *Precious*. For example, Bruce Baum (2010) discusses *Precious* alongside two other US films released at the end of 2009, *Invictus* and *Avatar*, arguing that, despite their differences, 'all three films convey the bogus idea of an already achieved post-racial America and a post-racial world. They all testify to a widespread desire – at least among white people – to pretend that a post-racial world has been achieved, or, alternatively, to deny that it has not yet been achieved' (2010: 636). As with Griffin, Baum notes how 'lighter-skinned (nearly white) blacks are upstanding middle-class Americans' (2010: 635) while 'the "blacker" characters in *Precious* are members of a self-sabotaging black underclass' (2010: 635). In other words, in a post-racial environment, where racism and racist thinking are understood – at least by white people – as things of the past, Precious' life involving rape, incest and illiteracy is presented as 'those of members of a black underclass and not primarily as due to racism and its legacy' (2010: 633).

In these arguments, the issue of the film's appeal to white audiences is significant. Jean-Charles discusses the relationship between the fantasy scenes and how 'rape is represented on screen through the use of the densely configured black female body – a black teenaged girl who is both dark-skinned and obese, aesthetic markers that should brand her body as abject according to the logics of normative white femininity' (2012: 143). She argues that the 'visual decadence' of the fantasy scenes 'privilege the audience's need for affirmative affective responses at the cost of elaborating a rape survivor-centred subjectivity' (2012: 143–144). Rebecca Morgan Frank (2012) unpacks not only the appeal of *Precious* to white audiences but also the condemnation it met with from Black male film critics. For example, discussing the author Ishmail Reed's critique of the film for offering white audiences a familiar stereotype of 'the merciful slave master' (Reed in Frank 2012: 217) in the form of the caring white characters, Frank argues that Reed focuses on the representations of Black men as sexual predators and thus 'deflects from race in order to focus on gender' (2012: 217). For Frank,

Reed's concern is not the experience or expression of black women or men, but how their experience is received and perceived. In his critique of the film, he is primarily concerned that *Precious* and *Push* undermine blacks by not offering the appropriate model of black life to white audiences. (2012: 217)[5]

As with Griffin, Reed sees *Precious* as organised around a white patriarchal and capitalist gaze, noting that '[w]hile [Reed] validly points out disturbing racial stereotypes and problematic scenes in the film, his focus on the white gaze renders not only the black woman, but the black woman artist, invisible' (2012: 217). Hence, Frank asks, 'What would happen if the white gaze were removed as the focal point, and the black male critic could look directly at the work of the black female artist without being self-conscious about the white gaze?' (2012: 218).

These arguments clearly indicate the tensions surrounding the film, its reception and place within wider cultural trends. For the purposes of this chapter's focus on the future politics of glitter, I want to return to the ways in which luminosity features in the fantasy scenes in *Precious*, what they suggest for the temporalities of the film and what light Black feminist theories shed on them. I also want to connect these with some scenes in *Glitter*, where luminosity is also significant in terms of how it configures race. Importantly, one way in which Griffin develops this account of whiteness as a dominant construction of privilege in the film is through the fantasy scenes, which indicate how Precious 'defines beauty and what she perceives as relief' (2014: 186). Griffin argues that Precious' fantasies are those of whiteness; in her fantasies she is accompanied by her light-skinned boyfriend, she adopts the movements and lifestyle of adored white celebrities and she is lit through bright and/or glimmering lights. For Griffin,

Reading Precious' imagined White female self absent a Black Feminist Theory lens, one might interpret her fantasy as innocent, since Precious knows she is not and cannot become the White woman she imagines in the mirror. However, it is essential to interrogate how Whiteness informs idealised femininity in a film that centres a Black female. More explicitly, why does imagining herself as a White woman offer Precious reprieve from the abusive horrors of her everyday life? From

5 Part of Griffin's argument here focuses on the representation of family in the film; see Mask (2012) for a discussion of cultural representations of the Black family in America.

a Black feminist standpoint, it is the imaginative quest for White beauty depicted that strengthens the dominant gaze. Thus, idealised White female beauty, read as in service to racism, colourism, and sizism, offers a means for Precious to look and feel better than her life allows for. In this vein, Precious can be understood as both a vehicle and agent of Whiteness in that the audience is transported into her escapist fantasy realm to bask with her in the glory of White femininity. (2014: 186)

Griffin here dislodges an understanding of Precious' fantasies of whiteness as 'innocent', arguing that 'idealised White female beauty' functions as racist and sizist and re-affirms for the (white) audience the superiority of whiteness.

Although, as I've discussed, it is a different kind of film, *Glitter* might also be understood in terms of the dominance of white beauty. The scene in which Billie is filming her video, which shows Billie seemingly happy and content, smiling with wonder at the glitter falling around her, for instance, is abruptly interrupted when she accidentally drops the fabric that has been covering her body and a shout of 'cut' is heard from the video director along with a ringing bell. As the director – a tall, slim white man – walks into the shot, he says, 'No, no, please. This is not working. The glitter can't overpower the artist'. The scene continues with the director – standing in between Billie's friends Roxanne and Louise, who continue to dance – saying, 'We ask ourselves, is she [Billie] white, is she black, we don't know. She's exotic. I want to see more of her breasts'. He shakes his head in despair at Billie's friends and, commenting to the record label manager, 'These girls are a joke. Get some strippers at least'. In this scene, Roxanne and Louise are depicted as incapable of matching up to the demands of the video director. They don't dance well enough – they are shown practising their moves – and neither do they look the part – they are neither sufficiently 'exotic' nor sexualised. Following Griffin's argument, they do not meet the white patriarchal gaze.[6]

The scene goes on to show the record company removing Roxanne and Louise from the video shoot and a struggle over what Billie should

6 Despite Billie and Dice's disapproval, Roxanne and Louise are dumped by the record label. In a scene that follows shortly afterwards, the three are shown on a shopping trip. After Billie assures them that they are 'family', they appear dressed in gold sparkly outfits carrying numerous shopping bags. Their relationship is reasserted through glitter.

wear for the shoot between Billie and Dice on the one side, and the record label and director on the other. While Billie and Dice protest about Billie wearing only a bikini, the director insists, 'I have to do my job, ok. Sex sells, she's hot, and that's how you sell records my friend'. At this point, Billie is introduced to her new publicist and her assistant, two white people whose style, both aesthetic and professional, is clearly at odds with Billie's. Running through her upcoming schedule, the publicist notes how Billie will not be doing photo shoots before 11am, as they want her to look 'fresh', and comments favourably on her outfit. Billie looks decidedly uncomfortable and overwhelmed throughout this exchange, which continues into the video shoot itself. Surrounded by four male dancers wearing body paint and not much else, Billie tries to avoid the dancers' groping until Dice halts the shoot and Billie and Dice walk off the set, to the exasperation of the record label.

The scene clearly sets up the ongoing struggle that Billie has between her growing success and keeping control of how she is treated and how her image is constructed. While Dice acts as a saviour in this scene, Billie rejects him later in the film after his own attempts to control her and her discovery that he has effectively bought her from her previous producer. Despite her music being firmly rooted in Black culture, from singing with her mother to her hits, which are influenced by disco and hip hop, Billie's exoticism is sexualised so that it becomes closer to what the white characters in charge of her image understand is successful. Her racial ambiguity is thus converted into 'sex sells'. Interestingly, in her role as Ms. Weiss in *Precious*, Carey's racial ambiguity is also introduced. Precious asks Ms. Weiss, 'So are you Italian or – what colour are you? Are you some type of black or Spanish?' to which Ms Weiss replies, 'What colour do you think I am?' In a discussion of how race features in Carey's career – including Carey playing the white rapper Eminem in one of her videos and commenting in 2009 after a reluctance to talk about race, 'I'm a black woman who is very light skinned' – Sika Dagbovie-Mullins (2013) suggests that 'Carey is at once definitely black, racially ambiguous, transgressing boundary crosser, and passer, both black and mixed race' (2013: 114).

As I noted above and in Chapter 3, luminosity is a technique through which young female characters are illuminated so that they stand out. In

Glitter and *Precious*, Billie and Precious become luminous through the various filmic techniques and conventions that I've discussed so far. What the discussion of race in these films points to are the ways in which luminosity and whiteness are connected. More than being simply present in the films, sparkle, shimmer and lighting are intimately tied to the ways in which whiteness – its dominance and its promise – becomes an organising principle of the films.

Fantasty, Fabulation, Futures

In Chapter 2, I introduced the concept of fabulation, which, in brief, refers to fiction or storytelling that nevertheless *feels real* in that it generates specific affective responses. Mullarkey notes that fabulation in Bergson's work refers to how fictions fabricate 'feel[ing] real emotions for unreal (fictitious) people and the events that befall them' because of how fiction makes these people and events 'come *alive* for us' (2007: 54). Deleuze (1995) puts a political twist on this concept by arguing that fabulation can be involved in creating a people who are missing. This is political because those who are missing are the minority, or minoritarian, and so fabulation creates alternatives to majority rule, producing the possibilities of different futures. He sees mediators – people and things – as crucial in this creative process. Here, I argue that glitter can be understood as a mediator of fabulation. Glitter brings alive fiction so that it feels real. The discussion of the way in which luminosity in *Glitter* and *Precious* functions in the service of whiteness demands a thinking through of how and for whom glitter brings these specific fictions alive. This is to respond both to *Glitter* bombing and *Precious* being a critical success for white audiences, and to how luminosity functions as a filmic technique that indicates the simultaneous possibilities and impossibilities of Billie's and Precious' futures.

To address both of these issues, it is helpful to note the ways in which some of the critiques of *Precious* are organised around unpacking and evaluating the film in terms of its representations. Mia Mask (2012), for example, agrees with Griffin that 'in Precious' mind, being a beautiful woman means appearing lighter-skinned than she is in real life' (2012: 99), and also argues that the film should be understood 'in light of the social, cultural, industrial, and most importantly, *cinematic* contexts from which the film emerges' (2012: 97). For Mask, it is crucial to note both how the film operates via a number of problematic stereotypes *and* how it is 'a complicated, albeit brutal, art film based on an African American woman's novel' (2012: 105). Mask's point in arguing for *Precious* to be understood as an art film is that it does not necessarily have 'an index-ical relationship to African American life' (2012: 105). She suggests that the film is 'realistic in terms of subject, surrealistic in terms of Precious' subjective experiences, and expressionist in the skewed configuration and lighting of the mise-en-scène and diegetic world' (2012: 105), and goes on to analyse some of the ways in which cinematic devices illustrate and emphasise Precious' 'longing, isolation, psychological dissociation and anger' (2012: 105). It is clearly important to analyse and intervene in the politics of representation in order to dislodge the ways in which whiteness dominates and structures the film's content and the ways in which audiences may be affected by it, as I have done so far. However, at the same time, given this book's aim to pluralise what politics might refer to and what it might involve and do, and to focus on future politics, it is also necessary to consider the ways in which the films may work non-representationally – that is, affectively.

Fabulation occurs through movement whereby the aliveness of fiction registers materially and perceptually. Fabulation is inventive. In this sense, then, indexicality, or the extent to which a film accurately represents real life, is one – but not the only – element of its potential power. Indeed, implicit in the criticisms of the affects of *Precious* on its white audience is an understanding that, despite the inaccuracy of the representations, the film is nevertheless significant – that is, problematic stereotypes of African-American men and women elicit affects in the white audience. Similarly, although critics panned *Glitter* for being 'an unintentionally hilarious compendium of time-tested cinematic clichés that illustrates the chasm between hopeful imitation and successful duplication', as the *New York Times* (Van Gelder 2001) put it, during the #JusticeForGlitter campaign, Mariah Carey's fans, the Lambs, posted clips from the film on Twitter and reasserted their love for it. Despite it not meeting the criteria of a finan-cially or aesthetically successful film, it nonetheless generates affective responses in some audiences.[7] While Griffin's argument, for example, is crucial in analysing the politics of representation, what is also worthwhile is an attention to what Katie M. Kanagawa terms 'its essential ambivalence' (2012: 118):

While scholars have emphasised the film's conservative *or* progressive social functions (i.e. its tendency to uphold hierarchical systems of difference or subvert them), what remains unexamined are the ways in which liberatory elements, such as the female protagonist's use of fantasy to lay claim to empowered agency and vice versa, thus rendering such either/or propositions and their attendant binary oppositions incomplete and somewhat beside the point. I argue that *Precious* cannot be categorised as essentially positive or negative in its approach to race, class, gender, and sexuality because it dialectically pairs forces aligned with sexist, racist, classist, and heteronormative systems of meaning (i.e. the status quo) with forces of resistance (such as Precious' empowerment narrative). As a dialectical narrative, *Precious* itself is a place where the progressive and the conservative come into contact and collide. (2012: 118)

Kanagawa's argument here resonates with that of Kokkola, discussed above, who argues that *Push* involves multiple and incompatible storylines of hope and despair. It also resonates with how I have analysed *Glitter* as featuring Billie in both painful and hopeful events.

Kanagawa develops her argument through an analysis of the fantasy scenes, and more specifically through the '[r]eality/fantasy pairings [that] constitute an important device that *Precious* uses to complicate the question of whether the film furthers the dominant cultural agenda or challenges it' (2012: 120). Refusing to see the fantasy scenes as either full of 'racial self-hatred' (Wellington in Kanagawa 2012: 120) or as in strict opposition to her 'real life', Kanagawa understands them as highlighting Precious' agency and empowerment. For example, she argues that, 'a simple dismissal of the power Precious achieves in her dream world as not real misses the extent to which Precious' empowerment narrative becomes less restricted to the fantasy world and increasingly takes place in reality, especially after she enrols in the alternative school, Each One

---

7 And, of course, the sneering that accompanied many reviews can also be understood as affective.

Teach One' (2012: 123). Moreover, the 'real-life' 'progressive empow-erment narrative of educational achievement and success comes to an abrupt halt after Precious receives a literary award' (2012: 130), when she learns from her mother about her father's death from HIV and is herself diagnosed with it. As such, the lines between reality and fantasy are not clear-cut, and Precious' empowered subjectivity 'must be continually asserted and reasserted' (2012: 130).

Kanagawa notes the importance of the lighting, sparkle and shimmer in *Precious*, discussing how it both marks transitions and moves between fantasies and scenes set in 'real life' – for example, in the literary award party scene, and in the final scene of the film, where '[c]lose-ups focus on her upturned, sun-kissed face, which is glowing with a sense of peace, hope and freedom' as she stands outside Ms Weiss' office with her two children (2012: 133). In so doing, Mask's point regarding the importance of the filmic conventions and techniques of *Precious* are highlighted. Kanagawa contextualises her analysis of the ambivalence of the film in academic work on girls studies, and particularly that on girl power (Aapola, Gonick and Harris 2005) and the 'can-do girl' (Harris 2004), which 'centre around the concepts of girls' agency, "control over the future", and personal accountability for their own success' (Kanagawa 2012: 131). This version of girlhood and neoliberal empowerment is problematised by girls studies scholars; Anita Harris, for example, posits 'at-risk girls' who are 'commonly associated with such social and moral concerns as teen pregnancy, sexual activity, sexually transmitted dis-ease (such as AIDS), drugs, violence, poverty, and so on' (Kanagawa 2012: 132). They represent, then, 'the remaindering effect of an exclu-sionary, thus oppressive, system of girl power' (Kanagawa 2012: 132). For Kanagawa, *Precious*

renders visible the non-traditional versions of girl power, paralleling some girls' studies scholars' efforts to posit alternative girl power narratives that break away from the normatively raced and classed paradigm and trouble the assumption that girl power narratives merely uphold the status quo. Precious, however fleetingly, envisions a girl power narrative for a so-called at-risk girl, mediating between discourses of female oppression and empowerment. (2012: 133)

This point, that there are alternative girl-power narratives that might, however fleetingly, indicate other possibilities for poor Black girls, is also picked up on by Kearney in her discussion of luminosity in the film. Recognising and agreeing with Griffin's identification of the white patriarchal gaze, Kearney argues that the fantasy scenes of Precious' 'internalised oppressions do not equate with its affirmation of the regressive ideologies supporting them. Rather, such fantasy sequences offer a critical lens by which viewers witness postfeminism's privileging of whiteness, thinness and spectacular glamour as well as feel its multivalent impact on *all* girls, even those like Precious who are not the primary target of such discourses' (2015: 267).

Kanagawa's and Kearney's arguments about the ambivalence of *Precious* and how the film works through multiple and incompatible storylines can be developed through a version of fabulation that accounts for, in Tavia Nyong'o's (2019) terms, 'the ways the study of blackness can rearrange our perceptions of chronology, time, and temporality' (2019: 4). Nyong'o posits a theory of Afro-fabulation, which works via an understanding of '*incompossibility*', or how a critical poetics of Black life 'tethers together worlds that can and cannot be, and is thus a necessary step toward investigating possibilities outside our present terms of order' (2019: 6). In different ways, in both *Precious* and *Glitter*, we see worlds that are both possible and impossible. In *Glitter* we see Billie's struggle to gain and retain autonomy over her body and career whilst having a loving relationship; her success in writing her own songs and performing at Madison Square Gardens is offset by the murder of her former partner Dice. In *Precious*, we frequently cross the uncertain boundaries between fantasy and real life, inner and socio-political life. In both we also begin to 'investigat[e] possibilities outside our present terms of order' (Nyong'o 2019: 6). The final scene of *Glitter* is a softly lit, glowing pastoral scene showing Billie, still dressed in her pale pink sparkly concert costume, meet and embrace her mother, after learning from a letter Dice wrote her shortly before his death that she is still alive and has not been drinking for many years. Billie is reunited with Lilian outside Lilian's home, which is surrounded by countryside. The contrast between this scene and the grey urban environment of their previous life together suggests new possibilities for them both.[8] In *Precious*, we

---

8 Although this better future works through a problematic depiction of the rural as superior to the urban.

might interpret the lead character's sparkling fantasy life as evidence not of a dupe's complicity with the racist, postfeminist, neoliberal regime, but of a survivor's creative negotiation of it via her envisioning of a better world based on the limited resources her mediated experiences have to offer. In other words, Precious' playful enactments of glittery celebrity function affectively as hopeful moments of what the good life might feel like. (Kearney 2015: 271)

Importantly, for Precious at least, the fantasised good life not only involves 'glittery celebrity' but also the desire *to be normal*. To repeat what Precious tells us at the beginning of the film: 'Every day I tell myself, something gonna happen, like, I'm gonna break through. Or somebody gonna break through to me. I'm gonna be normal. ... Someday'.

Lauren Berlant (2007), discussing the films *La Promesse* (1996) and *Rosetta* (1999), written and directed by Luc and Jean-Pierre Dardenne, describes the 'feeling of aspirational normalcy' (2007: 281), which is felt particularly acutely by those at the sharp or forgotten end of neoliberalism. It takes the shape of a fantasy, attachment or 'desire to feel normal and to feel normalcy as a ground of dependable life, a life that does not have to keep being reinvented' (2007: 281). Berlant explains how, for Rosetta, '[w]ithout membership in the army of labourers, she had no space for even a little cramped fantasy about spaces of the good life or good times ahead; now, with a job, Rosetta's fantasy is not at a grandiose scale but evokes a scene of an entirely imaginable normalcy whose simplicity enables her to rest unanxiously and, for the first and only time in the film, to have a good night' (2007: 275). Kanagawa notes how the first time we see Precious at Each One Teach One, Ms. Blu Rain 'extends her arm in a gesture of unconditional love and acceptance, inviting Precious to take a seat in front of the classroom (a space generally occupied, in her public school, by normal girls)' (2012: 127). We see Precious relaxing into the company and friendship of the other girls in the class, as well as in the home of Ms. Blu Rain and Katherine, and in various scenes with Abdul. While Billie's story is more spectacular than Precious' in that it involves her becoming a global superstar, there is also the persistent sense that what Billie also (really?) wants is to find love – as demonstrated in her comment to Dice that her success means nothing to her without him – and her mother. While in many ways these narratives reassert dominant versions of education, heteronormativity and the family, for those without them, they also hold the promise of rest and relief.

A prevalent way in which fabulation has been theorised is as the creation of an alternative future; indeed, in this book I have discussed and developed it in this way. The examples of *Glitter* and *Precious* complicate this understanding of fabulation by showing how the futures fabricated through fabulation may be not so much alternative or different as seeking to grasp and ground themselves in what is already possible or normal for many. In this sense, these futures may 'share in a coeval presentness' with what is now, as Nyong'o puts it (2019: 10); they both exist and do not yet exist, they are fantasies that are part of 'real life', blurring the boundaries between the two. Moreover, as Nyong'o argues,

Such black feminist and posthumanist acts of speculation are never simply a matter of inventing tall tales from whole cloth. More nearly, they are the tactical fictionalising of a world that is, from the point of view of black social life, already false. It is an insurgent movement – toward something else, something other, something more. While moments of afro-fabulation are indeed often ephemeral and fleeting ... they may also be ... monumental and enduring. Though neither may transform the conditions under which they appear, they live on through performative and narrative strategies and tactics that draw out of a black feminist and queer repository of counter-conduct, finding in collective memory an ever-renewing series of stratagems for aesthetic oppositionality. (2019: 6)

6

Sparkly Showers: Glitter-Bombing, Fabulation and Pre-Figurative Politics

as long as politicians continue their attacks on our communities, they can expect the sparkly showers to continue ... you can be certain I'm not the only one plotting fabulous future actions. (Espinosa 2017)

Glitter is a serious business for queer people. Glitter is how we have long made ourselves visible, even though becoming visible puts us at risk. (Edman, cited in Galli Robertson 2017)

During the 2012 US presidential election campaign, a number of Republican candidates, including Mitt Romney, Newt Gingrich and Rick Santorum, found themselves covered in glitter. LGBTQ* activists, protesting against homophobic and anti-choice ideas and policies, attended public events where the candidates were appearing and glitter-bombed them, throwing or sprinkling glitter over them. They often videoed the incidents and circulated them on social media. Other right-wing or transphobic public figures and institutions were also subjects of 'the sparkly showers', as Nick Espinosa, an equality advocate and activist who first conducted a glitter-bombing in 2011, puts it in the first epigraph above.[1]

In this chapter, I explore the affects that these and related glitter-bombings provoke, paying attention both to those elicited in the politicians, who often describe anger, annoyance and fear, and also those described by the LGBTQ* activists, who explain the glitter-bombings in terms of

---

1 It is worth noting that Espinosa features heavily in this chapter as media reporting of glitter-bombing focuses heavily on him. Espinosa wrote in the *Huffington Post* (Terkel 2011), 'It's surprising to see how many people have made the assumption that as a person who is fighting for LGBT equality I must be gay. I want to be clear that I am simply of a generation that will not tolerate bigotry and hatred toward any group of people. This is a basic human rights issue that I cannot ignore. It hurts me to see politicians who want to legistlate against love and prevent my friends from having equal rights to marry whom they choose, or to have the right to visit their partner on their deathbed'.

'sensational' and 'fabulous' ways to raise awareness of LGBTQ* issues and create change (Espinosa 2011, cited in Galli 2016: 269). Locating these glitter-bombings within a longer history of (sub)cultural activity and politics, I discuss the centrality of glitter in LGBTQ* culture, thus extending the focus of the previous three chapters from girlhood (broadly understood) to another minoritarian grouping. I draw particular attention to the material and affective qualities of glitter, and argue that the understandings and mobilisations of it as sensational and fabulous can be understood in terms of a future politics. In particular, I draw on Sontag's conceptualisation of Camp as both serious and frivolous, and I make connections between the idea of the fabulous and the concept of fabulation, discussed in Chapter 2, which is a process through which mediators create different futures. I then return to the glitter-bombings more specifically and see them as a mode of pre-figurative politics – a means of making the future in and as the present. Taking up Davina Cooper's (2013, 2017) working of pre-figurative politics into an understanding of everyday utopias introduced in Chapter 1, I see the glitter-bombings as a worlding practice, aiming to 'fabulise' the present (Ian 2011, cited in Galli 2016: 268) and in so doing to create a better future.

Glitter-Bombing, Activism and Affect

According to Anya M. Galli (2016), LGBTQ* glitter-bombings of right-wing people and organisations emerged as a phenomenon in 2011:

Activists first used a glitter bomb to protest LGBT rights in Minnesota, where seven of the eight incidences between May and October 2011 took place. Glitter bombing then spread to ten other states before returning to Minnesota in early 2012, when Republican candidates visited the state in anticipation of the February presidential primary election. Transgender rights activists also used glitter bombs to protest gay rights spokesperson Dan Savage's comments on transgender issues three times between November 2011 and February 2012. (2016: 267)

Espinosa describes the first glitter-bombing in 2011 as such:

My little sister and I skipped down a busy Minneapolis street giggling. Moments earlier I had opened up a Cheez-It box and showered glitter all over Republican presidential candidate Newt Gingrich. As the glitter fell I shouted, 'Feel the rainbow, Newt! Stop the hate! Stop the anti-gay politics. It's dividing our country, and it's not fixing our economy! (Espinosa 2017)

Espinosa goes on to explain how 'Security shoved us out the door, and we rushed home to upload the video from my sister's camera' (2017). As Galli notes, throughout the 2012 presidential campaign, a series of other glitter-bombings took place; indeed, it 'was hailed by one journalist as a "rite of passage" for anyone seeking the Republican presidential nomination' (Galli 2016: 267). Following the initial action in May 2011 involving Gingrich, other Republican candidates were glitter-bombed: Gingrich (again), Tim Pawlenty and Michele Bachmann in the autumn of 2011, and Mitt Romney, Ron Paul and Rick Santorum in the first few months of 2012. Rick Santorum, who in a 2003 interview said '[i]n every society, the definition of marriage has not ever to my knowledge included homosexuality. That's not to pick on homosexuality. It's not, you know, man on child, man on dog, or whatever the case may be' (*Washington Post* 2003), was glitter-bombed a total of six times (Galli 2016).[2]

It was not only people who were glitter-bombed. Other examples include a flash-mob dance and glitter-bombing at the Marcus Bachmann's Lake Elmo 'reparative therapy' clinic in Minnesota in 2012 (Galli Robertson 2017), organised by Espinosa. The activism was in response to comments by Marcus Bachmann – the husband of Republican presidential hopeful Michele Bachmann – that gay people are barbarians, and that '[b]arbarians need to be educated. They need to be disciplined' (Maffucci n.d.). Espinosa described to a local newspaper how a group of gay and gay-friendly activists dressed as barbarians checked first at the clinic that they would only be targeting staff and not those undergoing therapy, and then 'stormed the building, spreading glitter and joy' (Mullen 2011). In the days leading up to the 2017 inauguration of Donald Trump as President of the United States, a 'glitter-filled, rainbow-filled extravaganza' took place outside the temporary home of Vice President Mike Pence in Washington, DC (Galli Robertson 2017). Organised by WERK for Peace, an organisation led by Firas Nasr and established following the shooting dead of 49 people at Orlando nightclub Pulse, the activism was intended 'to send

2 For a timeline on glitter-bombings in the US in 2011–2012, see Galli (2016: 267).

a clear message to Mike Pence and other homophobic and transphobic individuals that this bigotry will not be tolerated in our country' (Nasr in Kelly 2017). While noting that the action let Pence know that 'we are there and we are watching', Nasr commented that it also involved 'celebrating our diversity by using our bodies to occupy space and love' (Nasr in Kelly 2017).

Incidents of glitter-bombing have also been reported beyond the United States. In October 2012 in Wellington, New Zealand, Germaine Greer was glitter-bombed by the Queer Avengers, a gay and transgender rights group who said of their protest, 'Transphobic feminism is so 20th century. Women's liberation must mean the right to refuse imposed gender rules, to fight for diverse gender expression' (*NZ Herald* 2012). In November 2016, ex-Labour MP George Galloway was glitter-bombed during a talk at the University of Aberdeen. In August 2018, a gay man, Nick Hurley, tweeted that he had glitter-bombed a car of boys who had shouted 'faggot' at him after he had picked up some glitter for Brighton Pride: 'If you think it's okay to shout "faggot" at me out of your car window while you drive past, then I think it's okay for me to empty a tube of glitter through that window when you stop at traffic lights. Your casual homophobia has supergay consequences [kissing face emoji, nail varnish emoji]' (Bollinger 2018).[3]

These examples serve to demonstrate how glitter-bombing emerged as a 'novel tactic' (Galli 2016) in LGBTQ* politics and activism; that is, while not 'entirely new to social movement repertoires', glitter-bombing can be understood as a 'tactical innovation' that 'provided momentum for activists at the same time that it motivated new responses from movement opponents' (Galli 2016: 260). Perhaps unsurprisingly, the glitter-bombing generated irritation, annoyance and anger in those who were targeted, and sometimes resulted in the activists being charged with criminal offences.

---

3 In an example that is purported to *be an incident of* rather than *protest against* homophobia, the desk of the only openly LGBTQ* officer in the University College London Student Union, Postgraduate Officer Mark Crawford, was glitter-bombed in March 2018, leading him to report that 'the homophobic intimidation tactic' had resulted in him 'fast reaching a point where I no longer feel comfortable coming to the office' (Bacon 2018).

Romney pressed charges against a Colorado student who glitter-bombed him in protest against his 'general political philosophy' (Coffman 2012). After his encounter with a glitter bomb, Gingrich opined that,

Glitter bombing is clearly an assault and should be treated as such. When someone reaches into a bag and throws something at you, how do you know if it is acid or something that stains permanently or something that can blind you? People have every right to their beliefs but no right to assault others. (Gingrich in Izadi 2015)

Galloway also framed his glitter-bombing in terms of an 'attack' on him. He tweeted that:

I know [sic] have an unknown substance in my eyes and lungs and feel a little unwell. But the struggle continues:-). (@georgegalloway, 21:10, 22 November 2016)

Galloway went on to say that he 'needed a good shower' (@georgegalloway, 01:29, 23 November 2016) to rid himself of the material and feel better.

These responses from those who were glitter-bombed are in contrast to the affects and emotions described by those who were involved in organising the glitter-bombing. For example, the action outside of Pence's home is framed in terms of celebration and love. Similarly, Espinosa described the glitter-bombing of the Bachmann clinic as 'joyous' and reported that '[m]ost of them had never participated in something like this. They said that it felt good – it felt good to stand up to the Bachmann's archaic views on LGBT equality' (in Mullen 2011). Media reporting of the glitter-bombings similarly focuses on positive affects. One report portrays it as 'an ingenious tool of protest. Its shimmery sheen carries an innocence and sparkling carefreeness' and notes '[i]ts association with fanciful things make glitter easy to dismiss as silly, random, even fun' (Basu 2015). The *New York Times* (Vinciguerra 2011) termed it 'a kinder, gentler pranksterism' and quotes the executive editor of the gay news magazine *The Advocate*, Diane Anderson-Minshall, as saying: 'It's peaceful and it doesn't hurt anybody. But it does get a really important point across in a fun way'. She goes on to note that, 'I think what you're seeing now is generational change. It's not more frivolous, but it is more lovely' (Vinciguerra 2011).

The Material Properties of Glitter: LGBTQ* Cultures of Protest

The affective qualities of glitter are discussed by Galli in terms of the importance of the 'symbolic power' of glitter (2016: 270). Galli's interviews with various glitter-bombing activists highlight how glitter-bombing was seen by these activists as 'lighthearted' and 'frivolous', making it 'attractive to movement newcomers and more experienced protestors alike' (2016: 269). For example, one member of a large organisation concerned with same-sex marriage and LGBT employment rights said that glitter-bombing was able to 'do a really great job [... at reaching] those people we're not going to be able to reach through traditional organising tactics' (David, in Galli 2016: 269). And despite the targets of the glitter-bombings reporting feeling scared, Galli suggests that,

> potential adopters initially perceived few, if any, risks associated with glitter bombing. When Espinosa chose glitter for the Gingrich action, he did so in part because glitter was lightweight enough that the action would be 'something confrontational that wouldn't be construed as violence' ... Activists were also careful to choose glitter that was large enough that it could not be inhaled or get into targets' eyes or airways. (Galli 2016: 269–270)

For those involved in Galli's interviews, care and attention was paid to the material properties of glitter: glitter was understood as 'lightweight' and thus not violent, and large glitter was selected so as not to inflict harm on targets. Indeed, Rachel E. B. Lang, a lawyer who glitter-bombed Michele Bachmann in June 2011, reported that a security guard who removed her following the action said, 'Thank you for using the large glitter' (Vinciguerra 2011). The large glitter was understood as not only less dangerous to health than the smaller pieces, but also less likely to stick on bodies, clothes and surrounding areas. Espinosa explained that another reason for his choice of glitter for the action on Gingrich was because 'I knew that it would stick with him and that, you know, for the days to come he'd be remembering what I said as he pulled the glitter sparkles from his hair. And that you know, of course, who doesn't want to see Newt Gingrich covered in glitter?' (Basu 2015). Picking up on this idea, one of the reports of a glitter-bombing of Romney describes how 'a gay rights activist who said he was from the group "Glitterati" threw a cup of glitter over the former Massachusetts governor. The glitter poured over his hair, stuck to his face and shimmered from his navy blazer' (Izadi 2015).[4] Also taking up this quality of glitter to stick and stay, the protests outside of Pence's house in 2017 were described as such: 'And because glitter is a delightful, vicious creature that will haunt you for months, one can only hope it'll leave a lasting impression on Pence and everything he owns' (Kelly 2017).

The paradoxical or contradictory nature of glitter – it is both 'delightful' and 'vicious' – is commented on in one of the epigraphs by LGBTQ* organiser and Episcopal priest Reverend Elizabeth Edman, who terms glitter 'a serious business for queer people. Glitter is how we have long made ourselves visible, even though becoming visible puts us at risk' (in Galli Robertson 2017). The decision to work with glitter to protest over LGBTQ* rights is not accidental, then; Galli notes that Espinosa selected glitter 'because it was "sensational", "fabulous", and "really resonated with the issue of gay marriage". His take on the novelty of glitter bombing was that it reached broader audiences by combining the "political moment" of the protest itself with the "cultural reference" of glitter and the entertainment factor of seeing a public figure "humiliated by something as harmless as glitter" ' (Galli 2016: 269). This 'cultural reference' to glitter is not expanded on by Espinosa but hints at Edman's point that glitter has a 'long' role in how LQBTQ* people might make themselves visible – a crucial political move but one that involves risk.

Galli contextualises glitter-bombing within popular and successful LGBTQ* 'performative protest tactics' in the US from the late 1960s onwards, some of which function through 'employing visual and attention-grabbing elements to draw attention to their cause' (Galli 2016: 261):

'Zap actions', for example, were disruptive public protests targeting politicians, medical professionals, and public organisations, and were designed to attract media attention rather than address specific political goals. Activists involved in 'pieings' of anti-gay public figures in the 1970s also relied on visual elements to transmit their message: the footage of Anita Bryant, leader of the antigay Save Our Children coalition, with her face covered in banana cream pie, remains a touchstone for the early fight for gay and lesbian rights in the U.S. Activists also used performance protest decades later when the AIDS Coalition to Unleash Power (ACT UP) carried out symbol-laden, confrontational protests against government inaction during the AIDS crisis in the 1990s. (Galli 2016: 261, references omitted)

4 Glitterati is the name Espinosa coined to describe glitter-bombing activists.

Galli's argument is important in understanding how glitter-bombing is a tactic in a social movement, and how this tactic has emerged through the 'symbol-laden' performative protests of longer LGBTQ* activism. What I want to consider further in the rest of this chapter are the material and affective qualities of glitter, and the role of glitter in the creation of a future politics. For example, as well as its visual elements being significant in protests, the role of glitter in wider LGBTQ* culture is also worth examining. That is, it is worth exploring in more detail what it is about *glitter* that makes it function as a performative LGBTQ* protest tactic.

Glitter, Camp and Frivolous Serious Politics

In her essay *Notes on Camp* (1966/2018), Susan Sontag describes 'Camp' as an 'alive and powerful' sensibility whose essence is 'its love of the unnatural: of artifice and exaggeration' (1966/2018: 1). She goes on to argue that, '[w]hile it's not true that Camp taste *is* homosexual taste, there is no doubt a peculiar affinity and overlap' (1966/2018: 30) and that 'homosexuals, by and large, constitute the vanguard – and the most articulate audience – of Camp' (1966/2018: 30). Sontag focuses her essay on Camp as a sensibility, a move she makes in order to express the difficulty of pinning down what Camp is. Camp, she argues, 'is almost, but not quite, ineffable' (1966/2018: 3). It is 'tentative', 'nimble' and changing (1966/2018: 3).[5] While she mentions the association between Camp sensibility and gay sensibility, this relationship is not expanded on. Moreover, Sontag argues that Camp sensibility is organised around aesthetics and style and thus, '[i]t goes without saying that the Camp sensibility is disengaged, depoliticised – or at least apolitical' (1966/2018: 5).

Matthew J. Jones (2016), who draws on Sontag's work to examine how Cunegonde's aria, 'Glitter and Be Gay', 'functions as a tool of queer resistance across the last half of the twentieth century' (2016: 422), argues that Sontag 'missed an opportunity to connect camp with queerness (or, for that matter, any meaningful political project)' (2016: 424). For Jones:

Camp is one of the most powerful tools through which gay communities perform ... transformative operations. Its plasticity – camp can function as noun, verb, and

5 Indeed, Sontag's essay is written as a series of notes or points, rather than in a more standard linear form.

adjective – evidences its fundamental role in 'doing' queer identities, and as a shared sensibility, camp marks the boundaries of a collective with shared or similar beliefs, ideologies, and political goals. (2016: 426)

Sontag's essay does not comment on glitter as an aspect of a camp sensibility, and Jones' focus is on versions of an aria performed at different points from the 1950s to the 1990s. Nevertheless, both of their arguments are productive for exploring the relationship between glitter and LGBTQ* politics. Jones argues that ' "Glitter and Be Gay" sings in multiple tongues: structural, musical, lyrical, and affective' (2016: 435), giving voice to gay listeners' 'own real life experiences of homophobia and the closet' (2016: 433) and 'encouraging future generations of gay men to find joy in their identity and love among their gay brothers and sisters. ... Glitter and be *gay*, indeed' (2016: 443). The relationship between glitter and LGBTQ* politics here, then, is described in temporal terms – as a process of giving voice or making visible present experience to transform it and create a better future.

Sontag's explanation of Camp as 'often decorative art, emphasising texture, sensuousness, surface, and style at the expense of content' (1966/ 2018: 6) resonates with the discussion of glitter as plastic in Chapter 2, and with the evaluations of femininity as shallow and superficial, explored in Chapters 3 and 4. In these ways, Sontag's argument would seem to be a critique of Camp, and, in the terms of this book, of glitter as well. However, although she problematically sees Camp as apolitical 'at least', Sontag's version of Camp resonates with the version of politics that I have been outlining so far in drawing attention to how that which is seemingly decorative and superficial might be involved in more critical matters. This is especially important to note in terms of minoritarian groups, which are those usually associated with surface, style and affect.[6] More specifically, Sontag's argument also connects with that expressed by the glitter-bombing activists. For example, Sontag delineates Camp as either naïve or deliberate, with the former being more 'satisfying' (1966/2018: 13). 'In naïve, or pure, Camp', she suggests, 'the essential element is seriousness, a seriousness that fails. Of course, not all seriousness that fails can be redeemed as Camp. Only that which has the proper mixture of the exaggerated, the fantastic, the passionate, and the naïve' (1966/2018: 16). Sontag's

6 On this point, see Taylor, Rupp and Gamson 2004; Taylor and Rupp 2006. Thanks to Anya Galli Robertson for drawing my attention to these papers.

framing of Camp here captures the contradictory qualities of glitter indicated above, as pointed to in Anderson-Minshall's comments about glitter being 'lovely' and Edman's comments about it being a 'serious business for queers'. Or, as Espinosa suggests, glitter is both fabulous and has the capacity to humiliate homophobes.

Further, a naïve Camp is a 'seriousness that fails'. This failure does not designate it as wrong or deficient; rather, '[w]hen something is just bad (rather than Camp), it's often because it is too mediocre in its ambition. The artist hasn't attempted to do anything really outlandish. ("It's too much", "It's too fantastic", "It's not to be believed", are standard phrases of Camp enthusiasm)' (Sontag 1966/2018: 24). Just as failure does not equate with being bad or inadequate, neither does success equate with being good or successful: 'Something is good not because it is achieved, but because another kind of truth about the human situation, another experience of what it is to be human – in short, another valid sensibility – is being revealed' (1966/2018: 24). Sontag argues that '[t]he whole point of Camp is to dethrone the serious. Camp is playful, anti-serious. More precisely, Camp involves a new, more complex relation to "the serious". One can be serious about the frivolous, frivolous about the serious' (1966/2018: 26).

Sontag's formulation of Camp as both serious and frivolous – or, more accurately, involving the serious being potentially frivolous rather than in opposition to it – can be readily taken up in relation to how glitter is understood by those who perform or are interested in glitter-bombing. Most obviously, Anderson-Minshall's comments, above, about glitter-bombing being 'not more frivolous, but ... more lovely' (Vinciguerra 2011) hint at both the playful and serious aspects of glitter-bombing. Anderson-Minshall's comments are included in a *New York Times* article titled 'Glittering rage' to support the journalist Thomas Vinciguerra's point that glitter-bombings continue a legacy of LGBTQ* protests, but in a calmer way. Comparing glitter-bombing to the more violent protests in the US, including the Stonewall riots in 1969 and those associated with the AIDS Coalition to Unleash Power (or ACT UP) direct action, Vinciguerra argues:

Now, as civil unions are busting out all over, H.I.V. is being brought to heel, and persons of different sexual orientations are assimilating into the American mainstream, glitter bombing is a decidedly less angry alternative. (2011)

Such a framing of the relationship between social change and the character of protests is also evident in Galli's work, which notes the correspondence between LGBTQ* rights being absorbed into legal and social areas and the professionalisation of LGBTQ* social movement organisations (2016: 261), and how glitter-bombing activists explain the protests as non-violent. This explanation of glitter-bombing as a 'lovely', 'less angry' form of protest fits into a mainstream progressive notion of history and social change, where rights are gradually won, equality spreads and things incrementally improve. The temporality of such an explanation is thus linear; the 'bad' past advances to a more adequate present and an even better future. The future is a time that is superior to the present and, hence, is distinct or separate to the present. While this is a widely accepted view of how time and social change works, it is problematic both in terms of seeing social change as inevitable, incremental and progressive (Foucault 1976/1998), and as understanding time as unfolding in a straightforward direction. As I have discussed in previous chapters, this book understands temporality as non-linear, the future as affective and capable of existing alongside or within the present and politics as multi-faceted and plural. In these senses, glitter-bombing as an attempt to bring about social change can and must be differently imagined.

Fabulation, the Extraordinary and Glitter as Political Mediator

Sontag's point about naïve Camp being 'a seriousness that fails' is helpful here. As I've discussed, Camp failure does not designate deficiency. Rather, Sontag argues that Camp 'is the attempt to do something extraordinary. But extraordinary in the sense, often, of being special, glamorous ... Not extraordinary merely in the sense of effort (1966/2018: 18). In Chapter 1, I discussed Bennett's idea of a naivety through which the human researcher may become attuned to the vibrancy and affectivity of things, and in Chapter 3 I developed this to explore how this might involve 'be[ing] struck and shaken by the extraordinary that lives amid the familiar and the everyday' (Bennett 2001: 4). While not entirely overlapping, Sontag's and Bennett's work point to the necessity of being open to the possibility of being affected – in Bennett's case by mundane and ordinary things, and in Sontag's case by that which is often rendered superficial and shallow. The extraordinary 'strikes and shakes' Bennett; Sontag describes that the reason for writing her essay is because 'I am strongly drawn to Camp, and almost as strongly offended by it' (1966/2018: 2). For both, then, in different ways, the extraordinary is vibrant and not necessarily defined by intentionality or effort.

In these ways, what Bennett and Sontag explain as the extraordinary may be understood in terms of the concept of fabulation. This concept, drawn from the work of Bergson and Deleuze, accounts for a kind of storytelling that is affective and future-oriented. Mullarkey explains that for Bergson, fabulation is how events come alive; both are made real and present via affect. For Deleuze, drawing on but also pushing Bergson's work, fabulation is 'the movement of constitution of a people' (1995: 125–126); a necessarily political process in that it is the creation of a collectivity that is oppositional to mainstream, majoritarian positions. Importantly, in contrast to social change as linear and progressive, fabulation creates futures through shock. Mullarkey, for example, highlights 'disturbance, shock or accident' as the 'stimulus' for fabulation (2007: 55). Without fabulation as 'the faculty of *seeing as*, we couldn't have the art that redeems the fragmenting activity of perception! The affect, or shock to thought which generates fabulation, which refracts our vision of the real, also creates the very same reality *effects* (or "illusions") that allow art to (in some degree, but never perfectly) defragment the real' (2007: 60). Mullarkey here draws attention both to the affect (as shock) that is inherent to fabulation, and to fabulation as 'seeing as', or as a representation or mediation. Fabulation is how fiction functions as 'very present and real' (Mullarkey 2007: 54). In this example, it is the affect of art that creates fabulation, so that art is understood not so much in terms of content – what it is of – as what it does – the sensations, perceptions and affections that it creates (Deleuze 1981/2007; Deleuze and Guattari 1996; see also Chapter 3). As such, as in Mullarkey's argument, the Hollywood blockbuster film *Titanic* is art because it generates the affects and perception in the audience that what they are watching is both fictional and real. It is movement that animates the present and that opens up a future.

Sontag's version of Camp, as an aesthetic style that is both serious and 'too much', may be understood as art in these terms. Indeed, as it is reworked by Jones in his discussion of music above, Camp may be this kind of fabulation in that it creates a queer collective and functions as a means of queer resistance. It does this through the combined style and affectivity of specific performances of a song, which register in the present and generate the sense of the possibility of a different and better future. As a movement that creates affects, percepts and sensation, art refers not only those practices that have traditionally been defined as art (such as painting, music, film, however contentious the boundaries of what constitutes high and more popular modes of these practices may be) but can also include popular culture (Coleman 2011). This is important to note, for it expands, or better pluralises, what might be considered political, for whom or what, and how. In this chapter, my argument is that glitter-bombing can be understood in terms of fabulation. It is an 'attempt to do something extraordinary' and thus is a mode of fabulation in its creation of 'a people to come'.

To consider glitter-bombing as art is to follow up on its emergence and framing as part of a longer history of LGBTQ* performative protest and the connection that I have made between it and Camp/camp. It is also to pull through the understanding of art as affect rather than in terms of whether it can be defined as 'good' (see also Chapter 3). Sontag's argument that 'something is good not because it is achieved' but because it exposes 'another valid sensibility' is worth considering in more detail here. Sontag explains this point through how Camp 'reveals' 'another kind of truth about the human situation, another experience of what it is to be human'. This is clearly crucial in terms of how glitter-bombing is intended to protest against and resist the attacks on LGBTQ* communities, as Espinosa puts it in the epigraph to this chapter, and at the same time to highlight to homophobes that the LGBTQ* community exists and celebrates its diversity, as Nasr puts it in describing the reasons for the protest outside Pence's home. However, in the terms of this book, glitter-bombing is an action that involves glitter as a thing – a material and medium. It is not only 'the human' that must be considered, then, but also *the things*. Furthermore, understood in terms of fabulation, glitter-bombing not only *reveals* a particular experience, but is involved in *producing* or *creating* it. Glitter-bombing is performative not only in its theatricality, but also in its enactment or invention of worlds.

Here, then, Deleuze's point that fabulation is created through mediators is helpful. Deleuze develops this point through reference to people, and especially artists, who work to create and establish alternative fictions that resist the mainstream and in so doing open up other, better, futures. However, he also notes that 'things too, even plants or animals' (1995: 125) may be mediators. Glitter, then, may be a mediator. It is vibrant and affective, and it is communicative and it mediates. As I discussed in Chapter 1, a key way in which I define glitter as a thing – that is, as both material and media – is through movement. The glitter in glitter-bombing is movement as understood through the concept of fabulation. It is creative becoming.

To develop this notion of glitter as a mediator in fabulation, this lengthy extract from Espinosa, taken from an article by him on the initial glitter-bombing of Gingrich, is instructive:

Why glitter?

What I have tried to do with creative forms of protest like glittering is to capture people's imagination and tap into a cultural point of reference with a piece of political theater projected into the real world. By creating a moment of conflict I shine a light onto the hypocrisy and bigotry of our current political discourse in a way that is as entertaining as it is dramatic.

As I have learned, creating a spectacle effectively engages the 24-hour news cycle and gives an opportunity to embed a succinct message in that moment. Social networks like Facebook and Twitter allow a short YouTube clip to go viral and reach audiences we would have never imagined.

The strength of glitter is that humor is an incredibly powerful tool for communicating a message – even a deadly serious one. We use humor to give hope to ourselves and each other, while contrasting our approach with the hateful and cruel attacks on our communities. (Espinosa 2017)

Here, Espinosa argues that glitter-bombing – or glittering – is 'a political piece of theatre projected into the real world'. As a mode of fabulation, glitter-bombing is both fictional and 'real'. It is also 'entertaining' as well as 'dramatic'. It is an affect that creates a 'seeing as'; it is a shock that opens up a queer sensibility. Espinosa explains these processes by highlighting the material and mediatic qualities of glitter. Glitter 'is' humorous and theatrical. It functions as serious-frivolous. It contrasts with 'the hateful and cruel attacks on our communities' through the spectacle of 'sparkly showers'. It 'gives hope to ourselves and each other'. Glitter is also 'an incredibly powerful tool for communicating a message', as Espinosa details with reference to social networks and digital platforms – and, it is important to note, to news media more widely. Glitter-bombing, then, 'serves a very specific purpose of bringing media attention and scrutiny to the bigoted views of anti-gay politicians. It will take all kinds of tactics and dedicated organising to win full equality', as he goes on to write. Glitter is also communicative in its orientation to that which is not yet, as Kember and Zylinska put it; it communicates here its desire to be involved in the achievement of a better future.

Pre-Figurative Politics, Presents and Futures

Espinosa's point that full equality is still to be won highlights the importance of the future politics of glitter-bombing (and of glitter more generally). Fabulation, as I've discussed, is a process of becoming. It is future-oriented, and in the work of Deleuze and those inspired by him, is also politically oriented. Hjorth describes fabulation as inventive of futures that change the conditions of the present for the better. A question that might be posed of glitter-bombing, then, is of how far the protests have been successful in meeting their intended aims of intervening in and altering discrimination and violence against LGBTQ* communities. Indeed, Galli argues that although glitter-bombing dispersed across the US in the months immediately following the action against Gingrich,

> its longevity as a method of protest for LGBT rights was very limited. Within a year of its emergence, the novel form of protest had disappeared from the movement's repertoire. The fact that celebrities were more likely targets for glitter bombs than politicians in the following year demonstrates that the initial excitement over glitter bombing as a novel social movement tactic was not enough to sustain its diffusion beyond early adopters. (2016: 274)

While Galli's focus is on glitter-bombing in the context of social movements concerned with changing party politics, and thus sees the glitter-bombing of celebrities as outside this remit or not as evidence of its decline as a tactic, her point indicates that the aims of activists were not achieved. Indeed, the election of Trump in the US in 2016 would suggest that the hateful, cruel and violent attacks on LGBTQ* and other minoritarian groups are in the ascendant. These are all important points to note; the achievement of better futures through progressive social movements are crucial. However, rather than working with a linear notion of time, progress and social change, instead I want to consider how the future politics that I am developing in this book understand temporality and change differently.

The idea of a future unspooling (seemingly) inevitably from the past and present is problematised in the concepts of fabulation and hope discussed above and in Chapter 2. Fabulation, for example, is described by Mullarkey as 'present-making': an actuality that happens now through movement, and that therefore animates a future. In ways that are similar but not synonymous, Muñoz's argument about hope that I introduced in Chapter 1 sees the future as illuminated and anticipated in the present. Hope is a potentiality that indicates both that 'the here and now simply is not enough' (Muñoz 2009: 96), and opens the possibility for a better, queer, future. In both of these accounts, the present and future are in non-linear relations with each other. The future is felt affectively in the present, rather than being a time separate to it (Coleman 2018a). What this suggests is that change is not only to be located in the future, but may also be being made in the present, or be present-making, in Mullarkey terms. Such an understanding of the future as in the present – indeed as part of what constitutes the present – also draws through my re-working of Sontag's point that 'good' equates not necessarily with success but with the creation of new sensibilities. Thus, what might be considered the 'failure' of the glitter-bombings in 2011 and 2012 to bring about a different future at the time of writing does not mean that they were deficient, unnecessary or incorrectly performed, but rather highlights the attempt to do something extraordinary rather than mediocre, to be unbelievable, 'too much', 'too fantastic' (Sontag 1966/2018: 16).

The extraordinary to which the glitter-bombings are oriented refers both to the means through which futures are made in and as the present and to the futures that are illuminated through these means. That is, the means and ends of glitter-bombings are both extraordinary: the glitter and the glitter-bombings are fabulous, as I have discussed, as are futures that celebrate diversity and create the space for love. In 'spreading … joy' (Mullen 2011) in the present, the glitter-bombings create joyous futures.

The ways in which the means and ends of glitter-bombings work together as present-making futures can be understood in terms of pre-figurative politics, which, for Cooper (2017), refer to the mixing together of means and ends so that the future that is desired is lived out within the confines of the present. The present and future are thus not collapsed into each other but are seen as in constitutive relations. Cooper's focus is on conceptual pre-figuration, which she defines in terms of working in relation to material practice. That is, she argues,

[a]gainst the assumption that more progressive conceptual meanings must await their right time and space, that they will follow the material practices such meanings are intended to 'capture', prefiguration is performative. It acts as if preferred meanings are currently operative, while knowing that they are not, both to reimagine what things could mean and to put new meanings into practice. Refusing the naturalised dominance of status quo understandings, conceptual prefiguration treats the terms through which everyday life and institutions are understood and enacted as if they could be otherwise. (2017: 336)

Conceptual pre-figuration does not come after material practices, but attempts to create material practices. It does this through knowingly acting *as if* preferred or alternative conceptual meanings were already in place. While my focus in this book is on glitter as thing – as material and medium – Cooper's argument about the relationship between conceptual and material practices within pre-figurative politics is productive for expanding an understanding of the future politics of glitter. What Cooper's argument suggests is that ideas, meanings and concepts work in tandem with, indeed are co-constitutive of, material practices. For the argument about glitter as pre-figurative politics, this suggests that the futures and presents, the means and ends, of glitter-bombing are intricately entangled.

Indeed, for Chris Dixon (2014), whose interest in pre-figurative politics has a much more practical focus in examining how politics is *done*, this entwined relationship between concepts and practice is also evident. 'For many activists', he writes,

the term 'prefigurative politics' has thus come to define a commitment to putting vision into practice through struggle. Sonya Z. Mehta, a former organiser with Young Workers United in San Francisco, succinctly summed up this understanding: 'prefigurative organising means organising now the way you want to see the world later'. The core idea here is that *how* we get ourselves to a transformed society (the means) is importantly related to *what* that transformed society will be (the ends). The means *prefigure* the ends. To engage in prefigurative politics, then, is to intentionally shape our activities to manifest our vision. (2014: 84–85)

Here, means and ends are explained in terms of the how and the what. How politics are done pre-figures what those politics will bring about. Furthermore, the ways that the how creates the what are present-making; they bring the future into the present. Cooper's argument also indicates that the ends do not necessarily come after the means but that the means create the ends now. Pre-figurative politics are not so concerned with 'await[ing] their right time and space', then, but with creating that preferred time and space in the present. Galli notes, for example, that 'Ian, a member of the "queer anarchist" group that used pink paint and glitter to vandalise the walls of the Human Rights Campaign building and store, said that the action symbolised his group's opposition to the organisation's "assimilationist" goals. Using glitter, he said, was part of their strategy to "fabulise the [HRC] building through direct action, making it, in our eyes, something beautiful' (Galli 2016: 268). The direct action to 'fabulise' the building that Ian describes both refuses a liberal assimilationist notion of incremental progression to a better future and creates a different and better future – making the building 'something beautiful' – so that the means and ends are conjoined in the now, creating or illuminating or fabulising an alternative in the present.

As a mode of pre-figurative politics, glitter-bombing 'undertak[es] what appears to be novel ... [and] provides a way of experiencing, demonstrating, and bringing into being its more developed (even institutionalised) future reality' (Cooper 2013: 82). It creates the world it wants to see in the present. The sparkly showers dramatize queer collectivity and spread joy. Glitter is fabulous and it fabulates.

Coda: Glitterworldings and Future Politics II

In the Introduction, I discussed Keeling's conception of the interdisciplinary scholarly imagination as an inventive endeavour, whereby futures that illuminate how things might be different are supported and created. Keeling argues that this is an interdisciplinary project because it draws on approaches that are appropriate for the things that are at stake in any study (rather than being a framework that already exists), bringing together multiple and what might be diverse and divergent streams of work. It is inventive because a particular field is assembled – temporarily and partially – and because new and particular questions and methods are posed and addressed. In its non-unification and open-endedness, this interdisciplinary scholarly imagination is future-oriented. It is also future-oriented because, as Keeling notes, other conceptions of the world – other worldings – become possible.

This book has sought to function in such a way: as an inventive endeavour through which a field is created – temporarily and partially – to understand glitter as it moves and worlds. Central to this endeavour has been the method of following glitter as a thing, and in so doing exploring practices involving glitter found in other worlds/worldings. What this book does, then, through a focus on glitter, is follow the worldings of glitter, concentrating especially on issues regarding the politics of gender, sexuality, race, class, age, bodies, (cultural and natural) environments and boundaries, filmic conventions, social change and progress, superficiality, frivolity, fun and seriousness, to name some of those explored. This method of following is partial and situated – it could not be otherwise, as Xin Liu (2019) argues. The ways in which glitter is followed do not mark the ends of glitter's movement, and it is notable that following glitter *as thing* can move quickly from its specific qualities and proper-ties to debates that it generates. Indeed, one of the main arguments of the book has been precisely to follow how glitter is involved in a range of politics that operate at a broad scale and are necessarily connected with other politics. Glitter could also be followed to worlds other than those examined in this book. I gesture towards some of these other worldings with the short interventions at the end of the book, which pose questions regarding glitter and a future politics. In this sense, the interdisciplinary scholarly imagination crosses and assembles various media and activi-ties, tracking where, when and how glitter is involved in illuminating instances through which a future that is somehow different to the now may be either or both present or possible.

The cases I analyse in this book are everyday, sometimes not that remarkable, as with vagazzling and vagina glitter bombs, which create moments of magic and wonder in otherwise mundane and usual situ-ations. They also centre techniques that may be overlooked, such as how glitter features as conventions that mark transitions between painful presents and different futures in the films *Glitter* and *Precious*. In comparison to, for example, the main narrative arcs or themes of the films, the actors who appear in them or their reception by critics and audiences, these aspects of the films have not received critical attention in and of themselves. More spectacularly, glitter-bombing becomes a mode of activism to challenge homophobia and bring about social change through making the present fabulous. In following glitter as it moves and worlds, one of my aims in this book has been to consider how 'the future' is at once imaginative – immaterial, perceptual – and material. Keeling writes of radical minoritarian movements including Black feminism:

The radical imagination works with and through what exists in order to call forth something presently absent: a new relationship between and within matter. It is radical because it goes against the root, taking aim at the very foundations of a shared reality. ... A marker of a historical mode of existence that exerts pressure on, and indeed has been perceived as antagonistic to, the ontology of the human, Black existence is a condition of possibility for moving beyond what is. At the same time, it presently anchors a set of possibilities for 'something else to be.' (Keeling 2019: 34)

Imagination, as it is expressed here, has the capacity to forge 'new relationship[s] between and within matter'. Matter, as I have suggested throughout the book, is lively, vibrant, transformational, and is, as Alaimo puts it, 'a subject of concern or wonder' and hence requires an attention to politics and ethics.

Keeling's formulation of the radical imagination here resonates with how imagination and the fictive are conceived in relation to fabulation. As I outlined in Chapter 1, to follow a thing is at once to be attending to its futures. Following is thus future-oriented. A key way in which I have followed the futures that glitter can make is through this concept of fabulation. Worlds may be worlded through fabulation as imagination, shock, wonder and enchantment, and through the entwinement of bodies and media, nature and culture, the serious and the frivolous. Fabulation is the process by which media that may not be real – such as Hollywood films and art – and mediators – which might be people or things – come alive. Fabulation is a political process or movement, whereby the majoritarian organisation of worlds is opposed and intervened in through the movement involved in the creation of a minority, of alternatives. I have argued that glitter can function as a mediator of fabulation, a moving, changing, processual thing – material and media – through which futures are made and the politics of making these futures are illuminated.

For example, vagazzling and vagina glitter bombs create moments whereby (straight, white) women transform heartbreak and 'the same old' lives and sexual encounters into enchanting experiences. Glitter-bombing embarrasses homophobic people by covering them in shimmer and sparkle, generating much media attention through the action. *Glitter* and *Precious*, to different extents, both put into play and question the possibilities of happy futures for the young Black and mixed-race women they depict, where whiteness, masculinity and middle-class values dominate, calling attention to precisely the need for new material relationships. These are all, I would suggest, hopeful activities and practices, in that in Muñoz's terms, they 'insist ... on potentiality or concrete possibility for another world' (2009: 1) because '[t]he here and now is simply not enough' (2009: 96). As Braidotti argues '[h]ope is a way of dreaming up possible futures: an anticipatory virtue that permeates our lives and activates them' (2013: 192).

However, these formulations of hope and fabulation do not guarantee success. As I discuss most explicitly in Chapters 5 and 6, the futures that glitter is involved in illuminating are not necessarily achieved. Despite imagining another world in her fantasies, Precious learns that she lives with HIV and her newly developed literacy will most likely not provide her with an income to support herself and her children. Billie Frank, the lead character in *Glitter*, finds fame and her mother at the end of the film, but endures the abuse and then murder of her boyfriend. The better worlds that are hinted at are at once present and still not-yet. The existing world persists. Indeed, in providing moments of wonder, vagazzling and vagina glitter bombs can shore up heterosexual relations whereby what matters is women's appearance and availability to men. In its demands for a world not only free of homophobia but also full of fabulous sparkle, the campness of glitter-bombing activism aims for the extraordinary – as Sontag puts it – and necessarily fails. Its ambition is outlandish, outstanding and, in the world in which it finds itself, it cannot but fail in the terms it sets itself. In failing, however, other sensibilities that highlight other possibilities are created. In understanding these activities in terms of their future politics, what I have aimed to propose in this book is that they, in Keeling's formulation, 'work ... with and through *what exists* in order to call forth something presently absent' (my emphasis). In this sense, they may be understood in terms of the pre-figurative politics that Cooper discusses, as concerned with 'what is doable and viable given the conditions of the present' (2013: 4) and as also, at the same time, illuminating and anticipating something else. In so doing, then, they indicate and construct a non-linear time, whereby the possibilities and potential of the future are at once not-yet and now – both present and (in) the future.

This book has followed glitter as a thing, noticing and exploring the practices through which new futures are imagined and materialised, are fabulated. I have argued throughout that glitter is a thing that is ubiquitous. It is and gets everywhere. As such, there are more glitterworldings to be made.

Fabulating

In a room at Goldsmiths in southeast London, around 20 of us work sepa-
rately and together with glitter. 'We' are a group of academics mainly based
in London including MA students, PhD researchers, early-career researchers
and more established lecturers and professors. We consider the properties
and qualities of glitter, the affects it elicits in us before, during and after we
work with it and some of the political questions it raises. Some report that
they came along because they love glitter, others that they have no strong
feelings towards it, and others that they wanted to participate as they were
intrigued by what would be involved in spending three hours working
with glitter. We put glitter together with 'natural' materials, including
leaves, wood and shells, and mass media including the free newspaper the
Metro *(owned by the same company who publish the right-wing tabloid*
newspapers the Daily Mail *and the* Mail on Sunday*) and magazines. Some*
of the glitter is newly purchased, some of it is biodegradable and some of it is
old and recycled from previous domestic and academic settings. We explore
how these different kinds of glitter draw us in or not. The biodegradable
glitter, for example, is popular but is worked with sparingly. It is expensive
and its environmentally friendly qualities encourage us to reflect on whether
or not to handle it, or waste it. The new and the old, recyclable glitter does
not attract many people. It appears garish and perhaps irresponsible in
relation to the biodegradable glitter, its artificiality apparent when next
to the 'natural' materials. We reflect on the politics and ethics of working
with a material that will find its way into landfill sites, waterways and seas,
fish and animals, endure for hundreds of years and pollute the planet. We
also contemplate what might be deemed the frivolousness and foolishness
of working with glitter in an academic setting that more usually involves
talking, listening and writing.

The workshop took place in late 2018 and was organised by Jayne
Osgood and myself as part of a series of events run by the Methods Lab,
Sociology Department, Goldsmiths, called 'How to do sociology with...' The

series explores how we do sociology with specific materials, devices, objects and atmospheres, and what happens when these things become the focus of our attention. In this case, we 'do' sociology with glitter, a thing that both Jayne and myself have been interested in and have written about from a feminist new materialist perspective (see Osgood 2019; Coleman 2019; Coleman and Osgood 2020).

This workshop is one of a number of workshops that I have participated in. In a workshop in 2018 with PhD students at Aarhus University, Denmark, organised by Britta Timm Knudsen and with Dorthe Staunæs, for example, we explored the kinds of research questions that glitter as an affective material might require us to ask, moving away from examining what a thing is to what it does and might do, for instance.[1] In a workshop in 2019 at Alberto Hurtado University in Santiago de Chile organised by Alejandra Energici, a small group of us worked with glitter to consider how visual and sensory methods involving materials might facilitate human participants to explore the relationships between body management and visual culture. In workshops in 2016 in London and Warsaw, Tara Page, Helen Palmer and I led exercises with groups of researchers where we contemplated through different practices the properties and affordances of various materials and media (see Coleman, Page and Palmer 2019).

Although different in focus, aims, structure and participants, what these activities have in common – for me at least – is an experimentation with what counts as knowledge making and a concentration on the methods, practices and things through which scholarly work might be done. These activities took place within academic settings – university seminar series, conferences and training schools – and involved (predominantly) academic researchers. They are also understood through my partial and situated position as an academic who works in a sociology department, albeit an interdisciplinary one; I am aware that in other disciplines, such a way of working and understanding knowledge production is not novel.

As part of the workshop organised by Jayne and myself, we provide print-outs of quotations from approaches that have inspired us in our understanding of glitter, and ask participants to contemplate them as they

---

1 Staunæs' contribution to the workshop focused on affective relations between humans and horses (see, for example, Staunæs' and Raffnsøe 2019).

work with the other materials. One of these quotations is from Bennett, who argues that,

Enchantment is something that we encounter, that hits us, but it is also a comport-ment that can be fostered through deliberate strategies. One of these strategies might be to give greater expression to the sense of play, another to hone sensory receptivity to the marvellous specificity of things. (2001: 4)

These workshops are an attempt to create the conditions through which 'to give greater expression to the sense of play, [and] to hone sensory recep-tivity to the marvellous specificity of things' (Bennett 2001: 4). Through the involvement of glitter in them, the workshops are one way in which I have attempted to practice an interdisciplinary scholarly imagination, working with people, approaches and things that come from various academic backgrounds and fields and worlding a way of doing (feminist cultural and new materialist) research. They provide opportunities to think and work with glitter, troubling the boundaries between producer and consumer, user and researcher, theorist and practitioner of glitter as participants fab-ricate shimmery artworks with glitter. The workshops therefore provide the conditions through which the future might be imagined and actualised.

Moreover, the processes through which these futures are imagined and fabulated are themselves temporary and open-ended; as Jen Tarr, Elena Gonzalez-Polledo and Flora Cornish (2018) argue, workshops are '"live" improvisational spaces' (2018: 40), which function in terms of uncer-tainty of participation, outputs and documentation. Not everyone likes working with glitter; participants in the workshops mentioned above have talked of the revulsion or anger they feel, others have noted its over-use in early years school settings, one declared that a friend had a phobia of it – sparkleophobia – and some have refused to touch it. A few months after the workshop in Santiago de Chile, Energici wrote to me saying that she was encountering a 'glitter resistance' in workshops she had organised with undergraduate students in critical psychology, as they selected materials other than glitter to work with. It is not always clear how workshops with glitter will unfold, nor the affects it might spark in individual and collectives of bodies.

Bennett argues that the conception of enchantment seeks to cap-ture how some things attract, appeal and fascinate. This enchantment is not necessarily or always positive, and when it is positive – in the sense of expanding the realm of what is possible – negative things may also emerge and exist at the same time. However, Bennett's argument here, as well as her work more generally, suggests the need to become receptive and attentive to ways in which enchantment may be encountered and experienced. Cultivating 'deliberate strategies' to do this 'becomes something like an academic duty' (Bennett 2001: 10). In a similar vein, I see the cultivation of strategies of fabulation to be something of an academic duty for those of us interested in future politics. These strategies would both provide opportunities for fabulation – as with the workshops – and become attentive towards how practices of fabulation already exist – as with the cases of activism, film-making and viewing, and the decoration of the inside and outside of the body discussed here. This twofold quality of the strategy of fabulation makes it possible to notice and understand how futures are being made, and how they might be made otherwise.

Interventions

Attuning

Glitter became intriguing to me in a number of ways. It struck me most explicitly following two workshops with teenage girls where they collaged imaginations of their futures. I noticed the glitter – became attuned to it – during the second workshop, when the bodies participating in the workshops and the classroom in which it was held became covered in it. I became fascinated with glitter and its movement around the space of the classroom – and beyond. After the workshops, on the bus to work with a large bag and a suitcase of left-over materials and completed collages, I noticed that glitter clung to my clothes and body. When I reached into my bag to make notes of a meeting with colleagues, I noticed that my notebook was also smeared in glitter. Transferring the materials and collages from the bag and suitcase into another bag in my office, I noticed the residue of glitter in the bag and suitcase – a feature the owner of the suitcase commented on upon its return, even after I'd tried to clean it off. The glitter followed me, and I followed it.

These short interventions gesture towards some of a plethora of other ways in which the future politics of glitter are being and may be fabulated.

Following

Figure 0.1
Glitter workshop, Body Management Project, Santiago de Chile, January 2019. Photograph by author.

* *What happens if we notice the various spaces and places that glitter moves to?*
* *What happens if we follow glitter to these spaces and places?*
* *What futures does following glitter generate? What futures does the glitter generate?*

Scattering

Figure 0.2
Blossom, 24 April 2019. Photograph by author.

This photograph shows blossom scattered on the ground of a street in south-east London. Its dispersal reminded me of how glitter scatters and spreads.

*   *Is the blossom waste?*
*   *Has it reached the end of its life?*
*   *Can it tell us anything about the problem of plastic waste?*
*   *What might be the futures of the blossom?*

Figure 0.3

How to do sociology with... glitter workshop, November 2018. Photograph by author.

In a chapter called ' "You can't separate it from anything": glitter's doings as materialised figurations of childhood (and) art', Jayne Osgood (2019) traces and reconfigures debates about childhood, contemporary art, gender, capitalism, the environment and activism through a focus on glitter. Discussing sustainable alternatives to glitter that are becoming increasingly popular in the cosmetics industry, she notes:

Children, similar in age to the excited girls in my fieldwork observation, are working in perilous, illegal mica mines. Illegal because they have been abandoned and/or collapsing. Bhalla ... reported the horror of this work: glittering practices that witness childhood encounters with mica include pneumoconiosis, a debilitating lung infection that can take up to 40 years to manifest. (Osgood 2019: 130)

What this one example indicates is that the production of mica glitter in these mines in India may help to produce a better future for the environment, but incapacitating futures for those who mine. Following sustainable glitter 'back' to its production highlights a 'sinister story, inflected with British colonialism and global capitalism' (Osgood 2019: 130):

Pursuing this string further reveals mica as a component in igneous and metamorphic rocks; first mined in India around 4,000 years ago when it was celebrated for its medicinal qualities. British colonisers discovered a substantial mica belt, and for many years the industry boomed across seven districts, with hundreds of legal mines employing tens of thousands of people (Bliss 2017). However, its decline generated acute rural poverty. Yet the global demand for mica continues and with it the emergence of illegal practices. Currently, 70 per cent of mica production in India is from illegal mines reliant upon child labour and exploited female miners. Glitter's doings in this specific space, place and time manifest in haunting, harrowing and frightful ways. (Osgood 2019: 130)

* *What futures might mica glitter generate, both for particular kinds of humans and the environment?*
* *What does the production of mica glitter suggest for the relations between particular kinds of humans and the environment?*
* *What are the implications of Osgood's argument for the development of a future politics of glitter?*

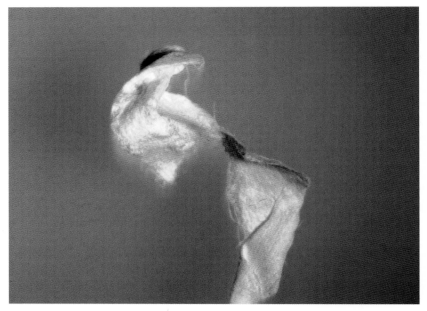

Figure 0.4

Max Liboiron, SP-31. Cod Sample #31, Saint Phillips, Newfoundland, 2016.

Photograph from Cod Objects (Ingestion Studies). Permission to reproduce this image kindly granted by Max Libioron. See https://maxliboiron.com/2015/12/31/cod-objects-ingestion-study (last accessed 26 July 2019)

Cod Objects (2016), by the feminist environmentalist scientist, science and technology studies scholar and activist Max Liboiron and her students, is a project in which they analysed the guts of 205 cod caught in Newfoundland, Canada, looking for plastic. This is a difficult task, as it is not straightforward to identify plastic from a range of other organic and inorganic objects that may have found their way inside the fish. This photograph is one of a series taken by the camera that is built into the microscope in their laboratory. The researchers ask: 'Is it plastic or not?' I do not know the answer.

In another art work, Plastic is Land *(2018), Liboiron notes that,*

plastic pollution, so often portrayed as a foreign invasion of nature, is part of the relations that make up landscapes. Originally from organic material, plastic polymers become part of the environments they interact with, including the inside of animals when plastics are ingested. In fact, one of the hardest and most time-consuming parts of laboratory studies of plastic ingestion is telling plastics apart from non-plastic look-alikes and act-alikes. This isn't to say that plastics are wonderful friends and we should all get along, but that Land is made of people, events, memories, animals, plants, air, spirits, soil, water, and since they were mass produced after 1945, plastics. (https://maxliboiron.com/2018/09/01/plastic-is-land-eider-ducks/, last accessed 26 April 2019)

Liboiron's projects are part of wider attempts to monitor marine plastic pollution and the harmful effects that this pollution has on various natural environments and species. A central issue that has emerged in these investigations is the traffic between organic and inorganic entities. Plastic, artificial although 'originally from organic material,' moves into other natural environments and, while not 'wonderful friends' with it, cannot be straightforwardly understood as 'a foreign invasion of nature.' Rather, plastic 'is part of the relations that make up landscapes.' Plastic generates a range of possible futures for 'nature' that unfold at different speeds and require different responses and modes of care (Gray-Cosgrove, Liboiron and Lepawsky 2015). Liboiron's approach to plastic resonates with that of Gabrys, Hawkins and Michael (Chapter 2), which draws attention to the plethora of future politics that plastic produce, and the need for these politics to be treated as empirical problems: what do plastics do in particular situations? Alongside the question of whether or not the photograph above shows us plastic, other questions might be posed.

* *If plastic is at once part of Land and damaging to Land, how might we disentangle the two? Would we want to?*
* *What role does the photograph, as a mediator of what is potentially plastic, play in its identification?*
* *What happens if a substance is identified as plastic? What futures does this identification generate? What worlds are fabulated? What happens if the substance is not identified as plastic, but as some other (organic or inorganic) substance? What futures are fabulated in these cases?*

Repeating

Figure 0.5

ART | 40 BASEL, Art Unlimited 2009.

Aluminum construction coated with impregnated quality craft papers, pneumatic fountain spray system, holographic laser-cut glitter, vacuum cleaning robots, LED illumination panels, wireless stereo speakers.

Photograph courtesy of :mentalKLINIK

The art work, Puff *(2009) by the artist duo :mentalKLINIK composed of Yasmin Baydar and Birol Demir, involves glitter being puffed out of three vents onto a raised floor as black disks continually clean it up. As the disks vacuum the glitter, more is produced. The audience watches this apparently futile repetition from around the edges of the floor. As they move, the disks make random patterns out of the glitter. The artwork creates what the artists call 'an unidentified space, an indecisive zone and a frozen time establishing various relations with materials and actions which construct an immaterial world' (:mentalKLINIK n.d.).*

* *Does this 'frozen time' involve futures? If so, how?*
* *What kinds of 'relations with materials and actions' are established? How are these material and immaterial?*
* *How does glitter act as mediator of these relations and times?*

Protesting

On 12 August 2019 in Mexico City, around 500 women gathered outside the offices of the Secretariat of Security and the Attorney General's Office to protest about two recent cases of alleged rape of teenage girls. The first case involved a 17-year-old girl who said that four policeman raped her in their control car in the north of the city on 3 August. The second involved a 16-year-old girl who said a policeman raped her in a museum in the city centre on 9 August. At the time of the protest, none of the policemen had been arrested or charged. The protestors called for justice for the two girls. According to the United Nations, nine women a day are believed to be murdered in Mexico. According to the Mexican Institute of Statistics and Geography, 44 per cent of women have suffered violence from a partner and 66 per cent of women have experienced some form of violence during their life (Oppenheim 2019).

As part of the protest, the walls of the buildings were spray-painted, and a pig's head was left outside the prosecutor's office. The security minister, Jesús Orta Martínez, was also covered in pink glitter.

Under the Twitter hashtag #NoNosCuidanNosViolan (They Don't Look After Me, They Rape Me), people posted pictures of pink glitter and wrote things including:

> *policeman are raping and assaulting women, yet the government believes that glitter used during manifestations is the problem.*

> *In case you didn't know a 17 year old girl was r*ped by 4 police officers in mexico city and they are walking free without any consequences but some women threw glitter at the sheriff and they're going under investigation but not the police officers*

> *Fight like a girl*

> *GLITTER MOTHERFUCKERS*

* *How is glitter a mediator of justice for these girls?*
* *What futures does the glitter-bombing seek to create?*
* *Can glitter here be understood as a mode of pre-figurative politics?*

Figure 3.1
Collaging workshop, 2016. Photograph by author.

Figure 3.2
Collaging workshop, 2016. Photograph by author.

Figure 3.3
Collaging workshop, 2016. Photograph by author.

Figure 3.4
Collaging workshop, 2016. Photograph by author.

Figure 3.5
Collaging workshop, 2016. Photograph by author.

Figure 3.6
Glitter collage, 2016. Photograph by Liron Zisser.

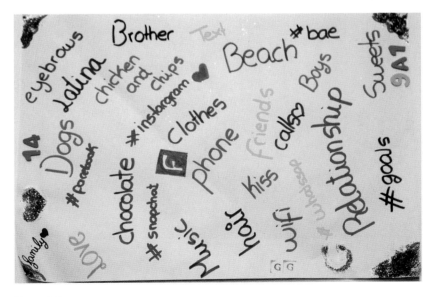

Figure 3.7
Glitter collage, 2016. Photograph by Liron Zisser.

Figure 3.8
Glitter collage, 2016. Photograph by Liron Zisser.

Figure 3.9
Glitter collage, 2016. Photograph by Liron Zisser.

Figure 3.10
Glitter collage, 2016. Photograph by Liron Zisser.

Figure 3.11
Glitter collage, 2016. Photograph by Liron Zisser.

References

:mentalKLINIK (n.d.) 'PuFF', www.mentalklinik.com/exhibition/puff/#0 (last accessed 6 November 2019).

Aapola, Sinikka, Gonick, Marnina and Harris, Anita (2005) *Young Femininity: Girl- hood, Power, and Social Change*, New York: Palgrave Macmillan.

Adams Media (2018) *Glitter: A Celebration of Sparkle*, London: Simon and Schuster, www. simonandschuster.com/books/Glitter!/Adams-Media/9781507208212 (last accessed 12 September 2018).

Alaimo, Stacy (2010) *Bodily Natures: Science, Environment and the Material Self*, Bloomington and Indianapolis, IN: Indiana University Press.

Appadurai, Arjun (1986) 'Introduction: commodities and the politics of value', in Appadurai, Arjun (ed.) *The Social Life of Things: Commodities in Cultural Perspective*, Cambridge: Cambridge University Press, pp. 3–63.

Armstrong, Isobel (2008) *Victorian Glassworlds: Glass Culture and Imagination 1830–1880*, Oxford: Oxford University Press.

Bacon, Lucy (2018) 'Desk of gay UCL officer glitter bombed after SU party in "homophobic attack"', March 2018, available at https://thetab.com/uk/london/2018/03/15/desk-of-gay-ucl-officer-glitter-bombed-after-su-party-in-homophobic-attack-31606 (last accessed 18 October 2018).

Barad, Karen (2007) *Meeting the Universe Halfway: Quantum Physics and the Entanglement of Matter and Meaning*, Durham, NC and New York: Duke University Press.

Barrett, Estelle and Bolt, Barbara (eds) (2012) *Carnal Knowledge: Towards a 'New Materialism' Through the Arts*, New York: I.B.Tauris.

Barrett, Estelle and Bolt, Barbara (eds) (2014) *Material Inventions: Applying Creative Research* , New York: I.B.Tauris.

Barry, Andrew (2005) 'Pharmaceutical matters: the invention of informed materials', *Theory, Culture and Society*, 22(1): 51–69.

Barthes, Roland (1957/2009) 'Plastic', in Barthes, Roland, *Mythologies*, London: Vintage, pp. 97–99.

Basu, Tanya (2015) 'Glitterbombs are back', in *The Atlantic*, www.theatlantic.com/politics/archive/2015/01/glitterbombs-are-back/384527/ (last accessed 1 March 2019).

Baum, Bruce (2010) 'Hollywood on race in the age of Obama: *Invictus, Precious*, and *Avatar*', *New Political Science*, 32(4): 627–636.

Bennett, Jane (2001) *The Enchantment of Modern Life: Attachments, Crossings, and Ethics*, Princeton, NJ: Princeton University Press.

Bennett, Jane (2010) *Vibrant Matter: A Political Ecology of Things*, Durham, NC and New York: Duke University Press.

Bensaude Vincent, Bernadette (2013) 'Plastics, materials and dreams of dematerialisation', in Gabrys, Jennifer, Hawkins, Gay and Michael, Mike (eds) *Accumulation: The Material Politics of Plastic*, London: Routledge, pp. 17–29.

Bergson, Henri (1977) *The Two Sources of Morality and Religion*, Notre Dame, IN: Notre Dame Press.

Berlant, Lauren (2007) 'Nearly utopian, nearly normal: post-Fordist affect in *La Promesse* and *Rosetta*', *Public Culture*, 19(2): 273–301.

Berlant, Lauren (2011) *Cruel Optimism*, Durham, NC and London: Duke University Press.

Bollinger, Alex (2018) 'After a group of men called him a "faggot", this guy set off a glitter bomb in their car', *LGBTQ Nation*, 6 August 2018, available at www.lgbtqnation.com/2018/08/group-men-called-faggot-guy-set-off-glitter-bomb-car/ (last accessed 18 October 2018).

Bogue, Roland (2006) 'Fabulation, narrative and the people to come', in Boundas, Constantin (ed.) *Deleuze and Philosophy*, Edinburgh: Edinburgh University Press, pp. 202–226.

Bogue, Roland (2010) 'Fabulation', in Parr, Adrian (ed.) *The Deleuze Dictionary*, Edinburgh: Edinburgh University Press, pp. 99–100.

Bolt, Barbara (2012) 'Introduction: toward a "new materialism" through the arts', in Barrett, Estelle and Bolt, Barbara (eds) *Carnal Knowlegde: Towards a 'New Materialism' Through the Arts*, New York: I.B.Tauris, pp. 1–14.

Boutet, Danielle (2012) 'Metaphors of the mind: art forms as modes of thinking and ways of being', in Barrett, Estelle and Bolt, Barbara (eds) *Carnal Knowledge: Towards a 'New Materialism' Through the Arts*, New York: I.B.Tauris, pp. 29–40.

Braidotti, Rosi (2013) *The Posthuman*, Cambridge: Polity.

Cagle, Van M. (2000) 'Trudging through the glitter trenches: the case of the New York Dolls', in Waldrep, Shelton (ed.) *The Seventies: The Age of Glitter in Popular Culture*, New York and London: Routledge, pp. 125–154.

Callon, Michel (1998) 'An essay on framing and overflowing: economic externalities revisited by sociology', *Sociological Review*, 46(1_suppl): 244–269.

Cashin, Declan (2017) 'Should glitter be banned? Scientists say glitter is bad for the environment, so should we stop using it altogether?', *BBC* 3, www.bbc.co.uk/bbcthree/article/e753478c-0396-4520-9646-e1aeca8f4b03 (last accessed 7 August 2018).

Coffman, Keith (2012) 'Colorado student charged in "glitter bomb" of Romney', *Reuters*, 9 February 2012, www.reuters.com/article/us-glitter-charges-colorado-idUSTRE8180AJ20120209 (last accessed 11 July 2018).

Clarke, Alison J. (1999) *Tupperware: The Promise of Plastic in 1950s America*, Washington, DC: Smithsonian Institute.

Coleman, Rebecca (2009) *The Becoming of Bodies: Girls, Images, Experience*, Manchester: Manchester University Press.

Coleman, Rebecca (2011) '"Be(come) yourself only better": self-transformation and the materialisation of images', in Guillaume, Laura and Hughes, Joe (eds) *Deleuze and the Body*, Edinburgh: Edinburgh University Press.

Coleman, Rebecca (2012) *Transforming Images: Screens, Affect, Futures*, London: Routledge.

Coleman, Rebecca (2014a) 'Habit, Temporality and the body as movement: 5:2 your life', *Somatechnics*, 4(1): 76–94.

Coleman, Rebecca (2014b) 'Inventive feminist theory: representation, materiality and intensive time', *Women: A Cultural Review*, 25(1): 27–45.

Coleman, Rebecca (2017a) 'A Sensory sociology of the future: affect, hope and inventive methodologies', *Sociological Review*, 65(3): 525–543.

Coleman, Rebecca (2017b) 'Developing speculative methods to explore speculative shipping: mail art, futurity and empiricism', in Wilkie, Alex, Savransky, Martin and Rosengarten, Marsha (eds) *Speculative Research: The Lure of Possible Futures*, London: Routledge.

Coleman, Rebecca (2018a) 'Affective futurity', in Sellberg, Karin (ed.) *Gender: Time*, Farmington Hills, MI: Macmillan.

Coleman, Rebecca (2018b) 'Pricing bodies: a feminist new materialist approach to the relations between the economic and socio-cultural', *Distinktion: Journal of Social Theory*, 19(2): 230–248.

Coleman, Rebecca (2019) 'Glitter: a methodology of following the thing', in Coleman, Rebecca, Page, Tara and Palmer, Helen (eds) 'Feminist New Materialist Practice: The Mattering of Method', Special Issue of *MAI: Journal of Feminism and Visual Culture*, May 2019.

Coleman, Rebecca and Osgood, Jayne (2020) 'PhEMaterialist encounters with glitter: The materialisation of ethics, politics and care in arts-based research' in Strom, Katie, Ringrose, Jessica, Osgood, Jayne and Renold, Emma (eds) 'Phematerialism: Response-able Research and Pedagogy', Special Issue of *Reconceptualising Educational Research Methodology*, 3(2), https://journals.hioa.no/index.php/rerm/index (last accessed 8 January 2020).

Cooper, Davina (2013) *Everyday Utopias: The Conceptual Life of Promising Spaces*, Durham, NC: Duke University Press.

Cooper, Davina (2017) 'Prefiguring the state', *Antipode*, 49(2): 335–356.

Cope, Andy and Oattes, Gavin (2018) *Shine: Rediscovering Your Energy, Happiness and Purpose*, Chichester: Wiley.

Dagbovie-Mullins, Sika (2013) *Crossing Black: Mixed-Race Identity in Modern American Fiction and Culture*, Knoxville, TN: University of Tennessee Press.

Davidson, Katherine (2017) 'Would YOU glitter-bomb your vagina?', *Daily Mail Australia*, www.dailymail.co.uk/femail/article-4759798/Mother-creates-glitter-bombs-women-s-vaginas.html (last accessed 11 October 2018).

Deleuze, Gilles (1995) *Negotiations*, New York: Columbia University Press.

Deleuze, Gilles (2003) *Francis Bacon: The Logic of Sensation*, New York: Continuum.

Deleuze, Gilles (1981/2007) *Francis Bacon: The Logic of Sensation*, New York: Continuum.

Deleuze, Gilles and Guattari, Felix (1987) *A Thousand Plateaus: Capitalism and Schizophrenia*, London and New York: Continuum.

Deleuze, Gilles and Guattari, Felix (1994) *What is Philosophy?* New York: Columbia University Press.

Despret, Vinciane (2004) 'The body we care for: figures of anthropo-zoo-genesis', *Body and Society*, 10(2–3): 111–134.

Dixon, Chris (2014) *Another Politics: Talking Across Today's Transformative Movements*, Oakland, CA: University of California Press.

Driscoll, Catherine (2002) *Girls: Feminine Adolescence in Popular Culture and Cultural Theory*, New York: Columbia University Press.

Dworkin, Craig (2013) *No Medium*, Cambridge, MA: The MIT Press.

Dyer, Richard (1997) *White: Essays on Race and Culture*, London: Routledge.

Edwards, Erica R. (2012) 'Tuning into *Precious*: the Black women's empowerment adaptation and the interruptions of the absurd', *Black Camera, An International Film Journal*, 4(1): 74–95.

Engle, Gigi (2017) 'Women are now using candy-flavoured glitterbombs to enhance their lady bits', *Marie Claire*, 10 July 2017, www.marieclaire.com/sex-love/news/a28155/vaginal-glitter-bombs/ (last accessed 12 October 2018).

Espinosa, Nick (2017) 'The glitter bomber speaks: a new generation feels the rainbow', *Huffington Post*, 10 March 2017, updated 6 December 2017, available at www.huffingtonpost.com/nick-espinosa/the-glitter-bomber-speaks_b_983331.html?guccounter=1 (last accessed 18 October 2018).

Featherstone, Mike (2009) 'Ubiquitous media: an introduction', *Theory, Culture and Society*, 26(2–3): 1–22.

Fotopoulou, Aristea and O'Riordan, Kate (2014) 'Introduction: queer feminist media praxis', *Ada: A Journal of Gender, New Media and Technology*, Issue No. 5.

Foucault, Michel (1976/1998) *History of Sexuality, Volume 1*, London: Penguin.

Frank, Rebecca Morgan (2012) 'A collective appetite: reception and the white gaze from Shange to Sapphire', *Black Camera, An International Film Journal*, 4(1): 215–219.

Frymorgen, Tomasz (2017) 'Doctors are warning people not to put this glitter capsule up their vaginas', BBC3 website, 29 September 2017, www.bbc.co.uk/bbcthree/article/fe30efb0-0b61-44f5-ac4f-41084820f7ad (last accessed 12 October 2018).

Gabbatiss, Josh (2017) 'Glitter should be banned over environmental impact, scientists warn', *Independent*, 16 November 2017, www.independent.co.uk/environment/glitter-ban-environment-microbead-impact-microplastics-scientists-warning-deep-ocean-a8056196.html (last accessed 3 August 2018).

Gabrys, Jennifer, Hawkins, Gay and Michael, Mike (eds) (2013a) *Accumulation: The Material Politics of Plastic*, London: Routledge.

Gabrys, Jennifer, Hawkins, Gay and Michael, Mike (2013b) 'Introduction: From materiality to plasticity', in Gabrys, Jennifer, Hawkins, Gay and Michael, Mike (eds) *Accumulation: The Material Politics of Plastic*, London: Routledge, pp. 1–14.

Galli, Anya M. (2016) 'How glitter bombing lost its sparkle: the emergence and decline of a novel social movement tactic', *Mobilisations: An International Quarterly*, 21(3): 259–282.

Galli Robertson, Anya M. (2017) 'Mixing glitter and protest to support LGBTQ rights', *The Conversation*, 13 March 2017, available at https://theconversation.com/mixing-glitter-and-protest-to-support-lgbtq-rights-74026 (last accessed 18 October 2018).

Goffman, Erving (1971), *Frame Analysis: An Essay on the Organization of Experience*, Chicago: Northeastern University Press.

Gray, Joanna (2018) *Be More Unicorn: How to Find Your Inner Sparkle*, London: Quadrille.

Gray-Cosgrove, Carmella, Liboiron, Max and Lepawsky, Josh (2015) 'The challenges of temporality to depollution and remediation', *Sapiens*, 8(1): pp. 1–9.

Griffin, Rachel Alicia (2014) '*Push*ing into *Precious*: Black women, media representation, and the glare of the white supremacist capitalist patriarchal gaze', *Critical Studies in Media Communications*, 31(3): 182–197.

Grosz, Elizabeth (1994) *Volatile Bodies: Toward a Corporeal Feminism*, Bloomington, IN: Indiana University Press.

Grosz, Elizabeth (2013) 'Habit today: Ravaisson, Bergson, Deleuze and us', *Body & Society*, 19(2–3): 217–239.

Gunter, Jen (2017) 'Don't glitter bomb your vagina', 2 July 2018, https://drjengunter.wordpress.com/2017/07/02/dont-glitter-bomb-your-vagina/ (last accessed 10 October 2018).

Hall, Stuart (1990) 'The emergence of cultural studies and the crisis of the humanities', *October*, 53: 11–23.

Haraway, Donna (1991) 'A cyborg manifesto: science, technology and socialist feminism in the late twentieth century', in D. Haraway (ed.) *Simians, Cyborgs and Women: The Reinvention of Nature*, London: Free Association Books, pp. 149–181.

Haraway, Donna (2012) *SF, Speculative Fabulation and String Figures*, Kassel: dOCUMENTA (13).

Haraway, Donna (2016) *Staying with the Trouble: Making Kin in the Chthulucene*, Durham, NC and London: Duke University Press.

Harris, Anita (2004) *Future Girl: Young Women in the Twenty-First Century*, New York: Routledge.

Harvey, Fiona (2017) 'Nurseries ban glitter in pre-Christmas drive for cleaner seas', *Guardian*, 17 November 2017, www.theguardian.com/environment/2017/nov/17/nurseries-ban-glitter-in-pre-christmas-drive-for-cleaner-seas (last accessed 7 August 2018).

Hawkins, Gay (2013) 'Made to be wasted: pet and the topologies of disposability', in Gabrys, Jennifer, Hawkins, Gay and Michael, Mike (eds) *Accumulation: The Material Politics of Plastic*, London: Routledge, pp. 49–67.

Hewitt, Jennifer Love (2010) *The Day I Shot Cupid*, New York: Hachette Books.

Heyes, Cressida J. (2007) *Self-Transformations: Foucault, Ethics and Normalised Bodies*, Oxford: Oxford University Press.

Hibou, Paisley (2011) 'A glimpse at glitter', *Quail Bell Magazine*, 5 September 2011, www.quailbellmagazine.com/the-real/the-history-of-sparkle# (last accessed 2 August 2018).

Hickey-Moody, Anna (2013) *Youth, Arts and Education: Reassembling Subjectivity Through Affect*, London: Routledge.

Hickey-Moody, Anna and Page, Tara (eds) (2015) *Arts, Pedagogy and Cultural Resistance: New Materialisms*, London: Rowman and Littlefield.

Hickey-Moody, Anna, Harwood, Valerie and McMahon, Samantha (2016) 'Feeling futures: the embodied imagination and intensive time', in Bland, David (eds) *Imagination for Inclusion: Diverse Contexts of Educational Practice*, London: Routledge, pp. 128–140.

Hjorth, Daniel (2009) 'Imagination – fabulation', Keynote Presentation at the ESU Confernece, Benevento, Italy, 8–13 September 2009, https://openarchive.cbs.dk/bitstream/handle/10398/8184/Imagination%20ESU%20conf.pdf?sequence=1 (last accessed 21 February 2019).

Hoffman, Jenn (2017) 'How a mother of three invented vaginal glitterboms and why doctors are warning against them', *New York Post*, 6 July 2017, www.news.com.au/lifestyle/relationships/sex/how-a-mother-of-three-invented-vaginal-glitterbombs-and-why-doctors-are-warning-against-them/news-story/2e39c1e00f0f1c6994c824474a8e04aa (last accessed 12 October 2018).

Hughes, Christina and Lury, Celia (2013) 'Re-turning feminist methodologies: from a social to an ecological epistemology', *Gender and Education* 25(6): 786–799.

Izadi, Elahe (2015) 'A brief history of politicians getting glitter-bombed', *Washington Post*, 6 March 2015, www.washingtonpost.com/news/the-fix/wp/2015/03/06/a-brief-history-of-politicians-getting-glitter-bombed/?noredirect=on&utm_term=.ca747706eaf2 (last accessed 11 July 2018).

Jean-Charles, Régine Michelle (2012) '"I think I was rape": Black feminist readings of affect and incest in *Precious*', *Black Camera, An International Film Journal*, 4(1): 139–160.

Jones, Matthew (2016) '"Enough of being basely tearful": "Glitter and be gay" and the camp politics of queer resistance', *Journal for the Society of American Music*, 10(4): 422–445.

Jones, Meredith (2008a) 'Media-bodies and screen-births: cosmetic surgery reality television', *Continuum*, 22(4): 515–524.

Jones, Meredith (2008b) *Skintight: An Anatomy of Cosmetic Surgery*. Oxford: Berg.

Jones, Meredith (2017) 'Expressive surfaces: the case of the designer vagina', *Theory, Culture and Society*, 34(7–8), pp. 29–50.

Juzwiak, Rick (2016) 'Where there aren't rainbows: examining Mariah Carey's *Glitter* breakdown 15 years later', *Jezebel*, 19 September 2016, https://themuse.jezebel.com/where-there-arent-rainbows-examining-mariah-careys-gli-1786645183 (last accessed 11 April 2019).

Kanagawa, Katie M. (2012) 'Dialectical mediation: the play of fantasy and reality in *Precious*', *Black Camera, An International Film Journal*, 4(1): 117–138.

Kavka, Misha (2008) *Reality Television, Affect and Intimacy: Reality Matters*, Basingstoke: Palgrave Macmillan.

Kearney, Mary Celeste (2015), 'Sparkle: luminosity and post-girl power media', *Continuum*, 29(2): 263–273.

Keeling, Kara (2019) *Queer Times, Black Futures*, New York: New York University Press.

Kelly, Hillary (2017) 'The glitter bomb dance party at Mike Pence's house tonight is the protest of our dreams', *Glamour*, www.glamour.com/story/the-glitter-bomb-dance-party-at-mike-pences-house-tonight-is-the-protest-of-our-dreams (last accessed 1 March 2019).

Kelly, Joan (1984) *Women, History and Theory*, Chicago: University of Chicago Press.

Kember, Sarah (2016) *iMedia. The Gendering of Objects, Environments and Smart Materials*, Basingstoke: Palgrave Macmillan.

Kember, Sarah and Zylinska, Joanna (2012) *Life After New Media: Mediation as a Vital Process*, Cambridge, MA: The MIT Press.

Kokkola, Lydia (2013) 'Learning to read politically: narratives of hope and narratives of despair in *Push* by Sapphire', *Cambridge Journal of Education*, 43(3): 391–405.

Kontturi, Katve-Kaisa (2018) *Ways of Following: Art, Materiality, Collaboration*, London: Open Humanities Press.

Knowles, Caroline (2014) *Flip-Flop: A Journey through Globalisation's Backroads*: London: Pluto.

Kwinter, Sanford (2001) *Architectures of Time: Toward a Theory of the Event in Modernist Culture*, Cambridge, MA: The MIT Press.

Lash, Scott and Lury, Celia (2007) *Global Culture Industry: The Mediation of Things*, Cambridge: Polity Press.

Law, John and Urry, John (2004) 'Enacting the social', *Economy and Society*, 33(3): 390–410.

Longhurst, Robyn (2001) *Bodies: Exploring Fluid Boundaries*, London and New York: Routledge.

Liboiron, Max (2016) 'Redefining pollution and action: the matters of plastics', *Journal of Material Culture*, 27(1): 87–101.

Liu, Xin (2019) 'Sensing smog on social media: rethinking tracing as the self-tracking of orginary humanicity', in Coleman, Rebecca, Page, Tara and Palmer, Helen (eds) 'Feminist New Materialist Practice: The Mattering of Method', Special Issue of *MAI: Journal of Feminism and Visual Culture*, May 2019.

Lury, Celia (2004) 'A more developed sign: the legal mediation of things', in Moran, Leslie, Sandon, Emma, Loizidou, Elena and Christie, Ian (eds) *Law's Moving Image*, London: The Glasshouse Press, pp. 209–224.

Lury, Celia (2012) 'Going live: towards an amphibious sociology', *Sociological Review*, 60(1 suppl): 184–197.

Lury, Celia, Parisi, Luciana and Terranova, Tiziana (eds) (2012) 'Topologies of culture', Special Issue of *Theory, Culture and Society*, 29(4–5).

Lury, Celia and Wakeford, Nina (eds) (2012) *Inventive Methods: The Happening of the Social*, London: Routledge.

Lury, Celia, Fensham, Rachel, Heller-Nicholas, Alexandra, Lammes, Sybille, Last, Angela, Michael, Mike and Uprichard, Emma (eds) (2018) *Routledge Handbook of Interdisciplinary Research Methods*, London: Routledge.

MacLure, Maggie (2013) 'Classification or wonder? Coding as an analytic practice in qualitative research', in Coleman, Rebecca and Ringrose, Jessica (eds) *Deleuze and Research Methodologies*, Edinburgh: Edinburgh University Press, pp. 164–183.

Malabou, Catherine (2005) *The Future of Hegel: Plasticity, Temporality and Dialectic*, London: Routledge.

Manning, Erin and Massumi, Brian (2014) *Thought in the Act*, Minneapolis, MN: University of Minnesota Press.

Marriott, James and Minio-Paluello, Minio (2013) 'Where does this stuff come from? Oil, plastic and the distribution of violence', in Gabrys, Jennifer, Hawkins, Gay and Michael, Mike (eds) *Accumulation: The Material Politics of Plastic*, London: Routledge, pp. 171–183.

Mask, Mia (2012) 'The precarious politics of *Precious*: a close reading of a cinematic text', *Black Camera, An International Film Journal*, 4(1): 96–116.

Massumi, Brian (1992) *A User's Guide to Capitalism and Schizophrenia: Deviations from Deleuze and Guattari*, Cambridge, MA: The MIT Press.

McRobbie, Angela (2009) *The Aftermath of Feminism: Gender, Culture and Social Change*, London: Sage.

McNeil, Maureen (2011) 'Post-millenial feminist theory: encounters with humanism, materialism, critique, nature, biology and Darwin', *Journal for Cultural Research*, 14(4): 427–437.

Meadowbrook Inventions (2015) 'What really defines a sparkle as "glitter"?', blogpost at: https://meadowbrookglitter.com/blog/what-really-defines-a-sparkle-as-glitter/ (last accessed 21 February 2019).

Meikle, Jeffrey L. (1995) *American Plastic: A Cultural History*, New Brunswick, NJ: Rutgers University Press.

Meikle, Jeffrey L. (1997) 'Material doubts: the consequences of plastic', *Environmental History*, 2(3): 278–300.

Michael, Mike (2012) 'De-signing the object of sociology: Toward an "idiotic" methodology', *Sociological Review*, 60(S1): 166–183.

Michael, Mike and Rosengarten, Marsha (2012) 'HIV, globalization and topology: of prepositions and propositions', *Theory, Culture and Society*, 29(1–2): 93–115.

Mirror, 'The Only Way is Essex's Amy Childs: "I'm the Vajazzle Queen"', *Mirror.co.uk*, 13 February 2011, updated 26 January 2012, www.mirror.co.uk/3am/celebrity-news/the-only-way-is-essexs-amy-childs-174991 (last accessed 4 October 2018).

Mitchell, W.J.T. (2017) 'Counting media: some rules of thumb', *Media Theory*, 1(1): 12–16, http://journalcontent.mediatheoryjournal.org/index.php/mt/article/view/13/9 (last accessed 9 August 2018).

Maffucci, Samantha (no date) 'Who is Michele Bachmann's husband? New details on Marcus Bachmann', *Your Tango*, www.yourtango.com/2018317464/who-is-michele-bachmanns-husband-new-details-on-marcus-bachmann (last accessed 1 March 2019).

Mullarkey, John (2007) 'Life, movement and the fabulation of the event', *Theory, Culture and Society*, 24(6): 53–70.

Mullen, Mike (2011) 'Nick Espinosa on Bachmann and Associates glitter-bombing', *City Pages*, www.citypages.com/news/nick-espinosa-on-bachmann-and-associates-glitter-bombing-interview-6559552 (last accessed 1 March 2019).

Muñoz, José Esteban (2009) *Cruising Utopia: The Then and There of Queer Futurity*, New York and London: New York University Press.

Nyong'o, Tavia (2019) *Afro-Fabulations: The Queer Drama of Black Life*, New York: New York University Press.

NZ Herald (2012) 'Germaine Greer "glitter bombed" by Queer Avengers', 14 March 2012, available at www.nzherald.co.nz/nz/news/article.cfm?c_id=1&objectid=10792049, (last accessed 18 October 2018).

O'Brien, Anna (2018) *A Life Full of Glitter: A Guide to Positive Thinking, Self-Acceptance, and Finding Your Sparkle in a (Sometimes) Negative World*, Coral Gables, FL: Mango.

Oppenheim, Maya (2019) 'Mexicans protest over alleged rape of teenage girls by police officers', *Independent*, 14 August 2019, www.independent.co.uk/news/world/americas/mexico-city-protest-police-rape-teenage-girls-demonstration-a9055641.html (last accessed 15 August 2019).

Osgood, Jayne (2019) '"You can't separate it from anything": glitter's doings as materialised figurations of childhood (and) art', in Sakr, Mona, and Osgood, Jayne (eds) *Post-Developmental Approaches to Childhood Art*, London: Bloomsbury, pp. 111–136.

Oyler, Lauren (2015) 'The history of glitter', *Broadly*, 14 September 2015, https://broadly.vice.com/en_us/article/3dxmp3/the-history-of-glitter (last accessed 21 February 2019).

Paasonen, Susanna (2011) *Grains of Resonance: Affect and Online Pornography*, Cambridge, MA: The MIT Press.

Paasonen, Susanna (2018) *Many Splendored Things: Thinking Sex and Play*, London: Goldsmiths Press.

Page, Tara, Palmer, Helen and Coleman, Rebecca (2019) 'Feminist new materialist practice: the mattering of method: introduction', in Coleman, Rebecca, Page, Tara and Palmer, Helen (eds) 'Feminist New Materialist Practice: The Mattering of Method', Special Issue of *MAI: Journal of Feminism and Visual Culture*, May 2019.

Papadopoulos, Dimitris (2011) 'The imaginary of plasticity: neural embodiment, epigenetics and ecomorphs', *Sociological Review*, 59(3): 432–456.

Parker, Laura (2017) 'To save the oceans, should you give up glitter?', *National Geographic*, 20 November 2017, https://news.nationalgeographic.com/2017/11/glitter-plastics-ocean-pollution-environment-spd/ (last accessed 12 July 2018).

Parikka, Jussi (2012) 'New materialism as media theory: medianatures and dirty matter', *Communication and Critical/Cultural Studies*, 9(1): 95–110.

Pass Notes (2018a) 'Angry about Brexit? David Cameron's smiling festival selfies definitely won't help', *Guardian*, 7 August 2018, www.theguardian.com/music/shortcuts/2018/aug/07/david-cameron-festival-selfies-wilderness-brexit (last accessed 24 April 2019).

Pass Notes (2018b) 'Glitter swimwear: you won't wear all of it for long, but you'll wear some of it for ever', *Guardian*, 15 May 2018, www.theguardian.com/fashion/shortcuts/2018/may/15/glitter-swimwear-you-wont-wear-all-of-it-for-long-but-youll-wear-some-of-it-for-ever (last accessed 3 August 2018).

Pratt, Gregory (2011) 'Bachmann & Associates visited by gay barbarian flash mob', *City Pages*, 25 August 2011, available at www.citypages.com/news/bachmann-and-associates-visited-by-gay-barbarian-flash-mob-photos-6540206 (last accessed 18 October 2018).

Savage, Mike and Roger Burrows (2007) 'The coming crisis of empirical sociology', *Sociology*, 41(5): 885–889.

Sciarretto, Amy (2013) 'Mariah Carey laughs at "Glitter", shades Eminem on "Watch What Happens"', Popcrush, 24 December 2013, http://popcrush.com/mariah-carey-laughs-glitter-shades-eminem-video/ (last accessed 11 April 2019).

Scott, Joan Wallach (1988) *Gender and the Politics of History*, New York: Columbia University Press.

Sedgwick, Eve Kosofsky (2003) *Touching Feeling: Affect, Pedagogy, Performativity*, Durham, NC and London: Duke University Press.

Serres, M. and B. Latour (1995) *Conversations on Science, Culture and Time*, Ann Arbor, MI: Michigan University Press.

Shildrick, Margaret (1994) *Leaky Bodies and Boundaries: Feminism, Postmodernism and (Bio)ethics*, London: Routledge.

Shove, Elizabeth, Watson, Matthew, Hand, Martin and Ingram, Jack (2007) *The Design of Everyday Life*, Oxford: Berg.

Sontag, Susan (1966/2018) *Notes on Camp*, London: Penguin.

Sparke, Penny (ed.) (1994) *The Plastics Age: From Bakelite to Beanbags and Beyond*, New York: Overlook Books.

Stacey, Jackie and Suchman, Lucy (2012) 'Animation and automation – the liveliness and labours of bodies and machines', *Body & Society*, 18(1): pp. 1–46.

Staunæs, Dorthe and Raffnsøe, Sverre (2019) 'Affective pedagogies, equine-assisted experiments and posthuman leadership', *Body & Society*, 25(1): 57–89.

Steinberg, Marc (2009) 'Anytime, anywhere: Tetsuwan Atomu stickers and the emergence of character merchandising', *Theory, Culture and Society* 26(2–3): 113–138.

Stewart, Kathleen (2007) *Ordinary Affects*, Durham, NC and London: Duke University Press.

Stoddard, Christine (2017) 'The history of glitter', *Huffington Post*, 6 December 2017, www.huffingtonpost.com/christine-stoddard/the-history-of-glitter_b_8941896. html?guccounter=1&guce_referrer_us=aHR0cHM6Ly93d3cuZ29vZ2xlLmNvbS88&guce_ referrer_cs=7Iny7eazejvG7mTavGBIJw (last accessed 21 February 2019).

Stoneman, Scott (2012) 'Ending fat stigma: *Precious,* visual culture and anti-obesity in the "fat movement"', *Review of Education, Pedagogy, and Cultural Studies*, 34(3–4): 197–207.

Suchman, Lucy (2007) *Human-Machine Reconfigurations: Plans and Situated Actions*, Cambridge: Cambridge University Press.

Swindle, Monica (2011), 'Feeling girl, girling feeling: an examination of "girl" as affect', *Rhizomes*, 22, www.rhizomes.net/issue22/swindle.html (last accessed 9 July 2018).

Tarr, Jen, Gonzalez-Polledo, Elena and Cornish, Flora (2018) 'On liveness: using arts workshops as a research method', *Qualitative Research*, 18(1): 36–52.

Taylor, Verta and Rupp, Leila J. (2006) 'Learning from drag queens', *Contexts*, 5(3): 12–17.

Taylor, Verta, Rupp, Leila J. and Gamson, Joshua (2004) 'Performing protest: drag shows as tactical repertoire of the gay and lesbian movement', in Myers, Daniel and Cress, Daniel (ed.) *Authority in Contention* (Research in Social Movements, Conflicts and Change, Vol. 25), Bingley: Emerald Group Publishing Limited, pp. 105–137.

Terkel, Amanda (2011) 'Newt Gingrich glitter prankster, Nick Espinosa, eyes 2012: GOP field is "ripe" for more stunts', *Huffington Post*, 18 July 2011, www. huffingtonpost.co.uk/entry/gingrich-glitter-nick-espinosa_n_863647?ri18n=true&gu ccounter=1&guce_referrer=aHR0cHM6Ly93d3cuZ29vZ2xlLmNvbS88&guce_referrer_ sig=AQAAAH8nFAtIumgWSWItb0pXsfHROhc3xXq9Xjnz7mJRfcUmag RUBm3lofHPEwqZOFoB-eckqcqJQshsp4c6-jL-RhmIw0h- I8hkhQTdKDKopLCDvFFWynajFGSkr6FiuTs88_eIq6ncm5M8MbD9Nkb9_ 1lUK6lCYsdo1qEYbnKMHF_K (last accessed 25 October 2019).

Thorogood, India (2016) 'What are microbeads and why should we ban them?', *Greenpeace. org.uk*, 14 January 2016, www.greenpeace.org.uk/what-are-plastic-microbeads-and-why-should-we-ban-them-20160114/ (last accessed 2 August 2018).

Van Gelder, Lawrence (2001) 'Film review: dreaming a dream and paying the price for it', *The New York Times*, 21 September 2001.

Vinciguerra, Thomas (2011) 'Glittering rage', in *The New York Times*, www.nytimes.com/ 2011/08/28/opinion/sunday/glitter-a-kinder-gentler-prank.html?_r=0 (last accessed 1 March 2019).

Washington Post (2003) Excerpt from the Santorum Interview, https://usatoday30.usatoday. com/news/washington/2003-04-23-santorum-excerpt_x.htm (last accessed 1 March 2019).

Weaver, Caity (2018) 'What is glitter? A strange journey to the glitter factory', *New York Times*, 21 December 2018, www.nytimes.com/2018/12/21/style/glitter-factory.html (last accessed 31 July 2019).

Wilkie, Alex, Michael, Mike and Plummer-Fernandez, Matthew (2014) 'Speculative method and twitter: bots, energy and three conceptual characters', *Sociological Review*, 63(1): 79–101.

Willingham, A. J. (2017) 'Glitter is not just annoying, it could be bad for the environment', *CNN*, 29 November 2017, https://edition.cnn.com/2017/11/29/health/glitter-environment-hazard-microbead-ban-trnd/index.html (last accessed 7 August 2018).

Woods, Faye (2014) 'Classed Femininity, performativity and Camp in British structured reality programming', *Television and New Media*, 15(3): 197–214.

Young, Sarah (2017) 'Doctors warn against new trend of women putting glitter in their vagina', 4 July 2017, www.independent.co.uk/life-style/women-glitter-vaginas-trend-doctors-warn-health-candy-scent-passion-dust-pretty-woman-inc-discharge-a7822461. html (last accessed 11 October 2018).

Index